Taylor Swift: Rise of an Icon – First Edition
© 2024 Future Publishing Limited

Future Books is an imprint of Future PLC
Quay House, The Ambury, Bath, BA1 1UA

The majority of content in this book previously appeared in *The Taylor Swift Fanbook* bookazine.

A catalogue record for this book is available from the British Library.

ISBN 9781805215240 hardback
UPC 1-95458-31543-8 01

The paper holds full FSC certification and accreditation.

Printed in China by C&C Offset Printing Co. Ltd. for Future PLC

Interested in Foreign Rights to publish this title?
Email: **licensing@futurenet.com**

Editor
Jacqueline Snowden

Art Editor
Katy Stokes

Contributors
Sarah Bankes, Ella Carter, Rachel Finn, Philippa Grafton, Amy Grisdale, Jessica Leggett, Kate Marsh, Carrie Mok, Dan Peel, Tiffany Starlow, Hannah Wales

Senior Art Editor
Andy Downes

Head of Art & Design
Greg Whitaker

Editorial Director
Jon White

Managing Director
Grainne McKenna

Production Project Manager
Matthew Eglinton

Global Business Development Manager
Jennifer Smith

Head of Future International & Bookazines
Tim Mathers

Cover image
Allen J Schaben / Los Angeles Times via Getty Images

Future plc is a public company quoted on the London Stock Exchange (symbol: FUTR)
www.futureplc.com

Chief Executive Officer **Jon Steinberg**
Non-Executive Chairman **Richard Huntingford**
Chief Financial and Strategy Officer **Penny Ladkin-Brand**

Tel +44 (0)1225 442 244

100% UNOFFICIAL

TAYLOR SWIFT

RISE OF AN ICON

WELCOME

For the past two decades, Taylor Swift has proven herself to be more than a musician. She's the voice of a generation, a role model, a cultural phenomenon – an icon. She continues to break records with her achievements, and has disrupted the music industry by forging her own path. It's little surprise she was named *TIME* magazine's Person of the Year for 2023. The ongoing Eras Tour is both a celebration of Taylor's sensational career so far, and a demonstration of her incredible performing power and influence.

In this book, you can relive Taylor's incredible journey from teen breakthrough act to global superstar. See how her music and style have evolved over the years, from her country roots, through *1989*'s synth vibes and the stripped-back indie sound of *folklore*, to *Midnights*' dreamy electro-pop. Discover how Taylor's personal life and relationships have shaped her songwriting, and how she uses her platform to support causes close to her heart.

At the time of writing, Eras continues to take the world by storm and fans eagerly await *The Tortured Poets Department*, so we also look to the future and consider what's on the horizon for Taylor throughout 2024 and beyond. Are you ready for it?

TABLE OF CONTENTS

12 CHAPTER 1
BECOMING MISS AMERICANA

28 CHAPTER 2
THE EVOLUTION OF TAYLOR SWIFT

112 CHAPTER 3
TEAM TAYLOR

132 CHAPTER 4
STYLE & SUBSTANCE

154 CHAPTER 5
SUPERSTAR

174 CHAPTER 6
ERAS & BEYOND

DISCOGRAPHY

38 TAYLOR SWIFT (2006)

44 FEARLESS (2008)

50 SPEAK NOW (2010)

56 RED (2012)

62 1989 (2014)

68 REPUTATION (2017)

74 LOVER (2019)

80 FOLKLORE (2020)

86 EVERMORE (2020)

92 MIDNIGHTS (2022)

TAYLOR'S VERSIONS

104 FEARLESS (2021)

106 RED (2021)

108 SPEAK NOW (2023)

110 1989 (2023)

CHAPTER 1

BECOMING MISS AMERICANA

BECOMING MISS AMERICANA

From a Christmas tree farm to the country music capital,
discover Taylor's journey to break into the business

B orn on 13 December 1989 in Reading, Pennsylvania, Taylor Alison Swift came into the world destined for greatness. Her parents gave her the androgynous name Taylor (after the American singer-songwriter James Taylor) in the hope that it might further her chances of success. Even as a tiny newborn, a bright future was already in the works…

Taylor spent much of her childhood in Wyomissing, Pennsylvania. She lived with her parents, Scott and Andrea, and her younger brother, Austin, at the family Christmas tree farm. "I had the most magical childhood," Taylor told *Rolling Stone* in 2009, "Running free and going anywhere I wanted to in my head." The family had horses too, which Taylor rode competitively, but she, like many other little kids, was also obsessed with fairytales, Disney songs, and – of course, inevitably – with music.

Taylor's maternal grandmother, Marjorie Finlay, was an opera singer. The Swift family have said that Taylor shared many qualities with her, and it was Marjorie who inspired her granddaughter to become a singer, something Taylor reflected upon on *evermore*. During a 2014 interview with *Esquire*, Taylor described her grandmother as beautiful and graceful – "She'd get up and sing, and, of course, it was the perfect, beautiful operatic voice. Gorgeous soprano."

The Swifts are a very close family. Taylor describes her mother, Andrea Swift, as her "favourite person in the world" and praises her for raising Taylor to be logical and practical in addition to shooting for the stars. Formerly a marketing executive, Andrea played a pivotal role in supporting her daughter as her career and fame snowballed, and helped to set up her daughter's MySpace page and website when Taylor's career was in its infancy. Taylor's former manager, Rick Barker, told *Entertainment Weekly* in 2008: "[Taylor's] mom and dad both have great marketing minds. I don't want to say fake it until you make it, but when you looked at her stuff, it was very professional even before she got her deal."

Taylor describes her father, Scott Swift, as "just a big teddy bear who tells me everything I do is perfect," also adding, "business-wise, he's brilliant." Yet when asked what it was like to manage their daughter's career, the Swifts are reported to have said that it was "just like soccer practice."

Supported by her family, as a youngster Taylor took to performing early. Andrea took her on regular trips to New York to see Broadway productions and she attended musical theatre classes. But it was singing that really became her passion. By the age of ten, she was singing at

RIGHT An 18-year-old Taylor on the red carpet at the 2008 MTV Video Music Awards in Los Angeles, California.

Wikimedia Commons/Shuvaev.

local fairs and events. At the age of just 11, she performed 'The Star-Spangled Banner' at a Philadelphia 76ers basketball game, receiving a standing ovation at the end.

At first, Taylor and her mother would make regular trips to Nashville so that Taylor could put her work in front of the labels and producers of Nashville's Music Row. "I took my demo CDs of karaoke songs, where I sound like a chipmunk," Taylor recalled in her interview with *Entertainment Weekly*, "And my mom waited in the car with my little brother while I knocked on doors up and down Music Row. I would say, 'Hi, I'm Taylor. I'm 11; I want a record deal. Call me.'"

But when the phone wasn't ringing for her demos of cover songs, Taylor quickly realised that the way to make her mark would be to start writing original material.

— ✦ —

ABOVE Taylor's childhood home in Wyomissing, PA, where the Swift family lived before moving to Tennessee.

LEFT A young Taylor performing the national anthem at a World Series game in 2008.

In the same *Entertainment Weekly* interview from 2008, Andrea Swift described the first time her 12-year-old daughter came across a 12-string guitar: "She thought it was the coolest thing." Taylor is famously stubborn and driven, and so even then this became a project to overcome and to prove that she was worthy of stardom. Her mother continued, "Of course we immediately said, 'Oh no, your fingers are too small.' Well, that was all it took. Don't ever say 'never' or 'can't do' to Taylor. She started playing it four hours a day."

Netflix's 2020 documentary, *Miss Americana*, explores Taylor's journey to stardom and offers a rare glimpse into her and her family's day-to-day lives. Footage of a young tween Taylor shows her performing at various events with the confidence of a seasoned pro, while other clips show her performing original songs at home on her guitar.

During one of these home video performances, a young Taylor introduces one original song by describing it as "about a girl who's just… different." She began writing songs by telling stories about her experiences and emotions, and it's a tradition that has continued throughout her expansive career. "I never felt like the kids in school were

> ## "When Taylor was 14, the entire family made the pivotal decision to leave Pennsylvania and made a new life in Tennessee"

— ✦ —

right about me when they'd say, 'She's weird. She's annoying. I don't want to hang out with her,'" Taylor explained in an interview with *Esquire* in 2014. "I always remember writing in my journal, saying, I just have to keep writing songs. I just have to keep doing this and someday, maybe, this will be different for me. I just have to keep working."

A fiercely determined kid and a self-confessed perfectionist, this mantra would indeed become a reality. Taylor's main inspiration for songwriting is rooted in country music, and her love for the genre was sparked when her parents took her to see LeAnn Rimes in concert at six years old.

From there, Taylor looked up to classic country singers such as Dolly Parton and Patsy Cline. She has said she was greatly influenced by "the great female country artists of the 90s". Shania Twain was a huge source of inspiration, Faith Hill was her idol for everything, from music to fashion, and she admired The Chicks for their sheer attitude and their ability to play their own instruments. A whole host of other artists contributed to her melting pot of inspiration (she was and still is a huge Britney Spears fan), but it was through country that Taylor chose to make her mark on the music industry.

"Country music teaches you to work," Taylor explained in the *Esquire* interview. "I've never been more proud to have come from a community that's so rooted in songwriting, so rooted in hard work and in treating people well. It was the best kind of training."

And hard work is precisely what Taylor and her family put in. At age 13, Taylor landed a spot on an artist development programme with RCA Records in Nashville, but this only lasted for a year. She decided to opt out of renewing the deal, as she was laser-focused on her dream of writing and recording her own material.

"It's not a really popular thing to do in Nashville, to walk away from a major record deal," Taylor admitted in an interview with *Entertainment Weekly* in 2007, "But that's what I did, because I wanted to find some place that would really put a lot of time and care into this." She continued, "I didn't want to just be another girl singer. I wanted there to

be something that set me apart. And I knew that had to be my writing."

It was this desire to write and perform original material that led her to become the youngest person to ever sign as a songwriter with Sony/ATV Publishing at the age of 14.

Spurred on by her ultra-determined goal, it became apparent to the Swift family that Taylor's career needed more than just regular trips to the renowned Music City, a hub for artists and record labels, also known as 'The Songwriting Capital of the World'. Her parents were adamant that they should support their daughter in her goal of becoming a recording artist, while at the same time offering her as 'normal' a life as possible. So when Taylor was 14, the entire family made the pivotal decision to leave their home on the Christmas tree farm in Pennsylvania and made a new life in Hendersonville, Tennessee – a town about 20 minutes north of Nashville.

Once fully immersed in the Nashville music scene, Taylor began working even harder to showcase her talent. At a writers' round, where songwriters get together to perform their material, she met Liz Rose – one of Nashville's songwriting heavyweights. Rose would go on to become Taylor's co-writer for her early albums, and in an interview with *The Washington Post* in 2016, she described their collaborative sessions as "the easiest, funnest thing I [did] all week". Such was Taylor's flair for songwriting, Rose added, "The first time we wrote, I walked out and said, 'I don't know what I was doing there,' she really didn't need me."

Nashville life afforded Taylor many of these crucial introductions into the industry that she loved. In addition to her songwriting collaborations, she continued to make CDs and demos and sent them out to labels in order to find the right platform to launch what would turn into an exceptional, award-winning career.

— ✦ —

RIGHT "This is definitely the highlight of my senior year!" Taylor exclaimed when receiving the CMA Horizon Award in 2007.

COUNTRY MUSIC ASSOCIATION AWARDS | TENNESSEE | 07 NOV 2007

"When you're singing, you
can hear the echo of people
in the audience singing
every single word with you,
and that was that big dream
that I had for myself."

—✦—

LEFT Taylor performing on stage in Kansas City, 11 May 2007.

One such package landed on the desk of Scott Borchetta, a record executive who at the time was working for Universal Records. Talking on *Larry King Now*, Borchetta revealed how he went to see her perform at the Bluebird Cafe. An unassuming venue set in a strip mall outside downtown Nashville, the Bluebird Cafe is a music industry institution, where the 90 seats are filled night after night with people eager to hear artists perform original work. In November 2014, a 15-year-old Taylor Swift was one of these performers, and after her set, Borchetta met with her and her family.

They got on well, and despite offering to provide an intro to Universal Records, Taylor put her faith in Borchetta as he set up his own label – Big Machine Records. "I felt like I needed my own direction and the kind of attention that a little label will give you," Taylor told *Entertainment Weekly* in 2007, "I wanted a record label that needed me, that absolutely was counting on me to succeed. I love that pressure." The label would go on to support her through six albums, before a huge battle over Taylor's master recording rights would eventually turn the relationship sour.

Under Big Machine, Taylor recorded her debut self-titled album, which launched on 24 October 2006. With 11 original tracks that she had either self-penned or co-written, five were released as singles – the first of which was 'Tim McGraw'. Named after and inspired by the songs of one of her favourite country musicians, this first single was a great example of Taylor's personal songwriting style. She confesses that she wrote it while thinking about her feelings for a boy she was dating at the time. Of the writing process, she admitted later that "the idea for this song came to me in math class. I just started singing to myself."

Catchy and quintessentially Taylor, 'Tim McGraw' peaked at number six on the Country Charts and reached number 33 in the *Billboard* Hot 100, firmly rooting Taylor

— ✦ —

RIGHT Taylor pictured backstage with her mother and father in 2013. "My parents moved across the country so I could pursue a dream," she reflected in a 2008 interview with *Blender*.

BELOW Taylor with her younger brother, Austin, in 2009.

Andrew Walker/DCPNYE/Getty Images.

"Throughout her early
success, Taylor was
capturing fans with
her down-to-earth and
occasionally goofy
teenage realness"

— ✦ —

as a promising young artist to watch. Effortlessly bridging
the gap between country music and mainstream pop, by
the end of 2007 Taylor's eponymous debut record had gone
platinum, selling over 1 million copies in the United States
alone. She had the 19th best-selling album of the year and
became the 10th best-selling female artist of the year – all
without even having finished high school. After taking
home the Horizon Award at the Country Music Association
Awards in November 2007, Taylor famously exclaimed,
"This is definitely the highlight of my senior year!"

Throughout all of this early success, Taylor was capturing
fans with her down-to-earth and occasionally goofy teenage
realness. With literally millions and millions of MySpace
song streams, she was being herself online at a time when
social media was in its infancy, and to her fans she was
both accessible and relatable. "I'm just a teenager, you
know?" she told *The Washington Post* in 2008. "I'm not
going to try to act like some adult who has it all together
and isn't fazed at all by that."

With the success of her debut album, Taylor began a
huge touring schedule, opening the show for top country
artists Faith Hill and Tim McGraw on their Soul2Soul II
tour in 2007. While juggling performances and school
work on the road, she was also writing new material, ideas
already flowing for her next album. By the time she was
18, Taylor was making a living from music just like she'd
always dreamed, and yet that was only the beginning of her
incredible career to come.

— ✦ —

LEFT Taylor celebrating with fellow celebrity guests on *Dick Clark's
New Year's Rockin' Eve 2009* with Ryan Seacrest.

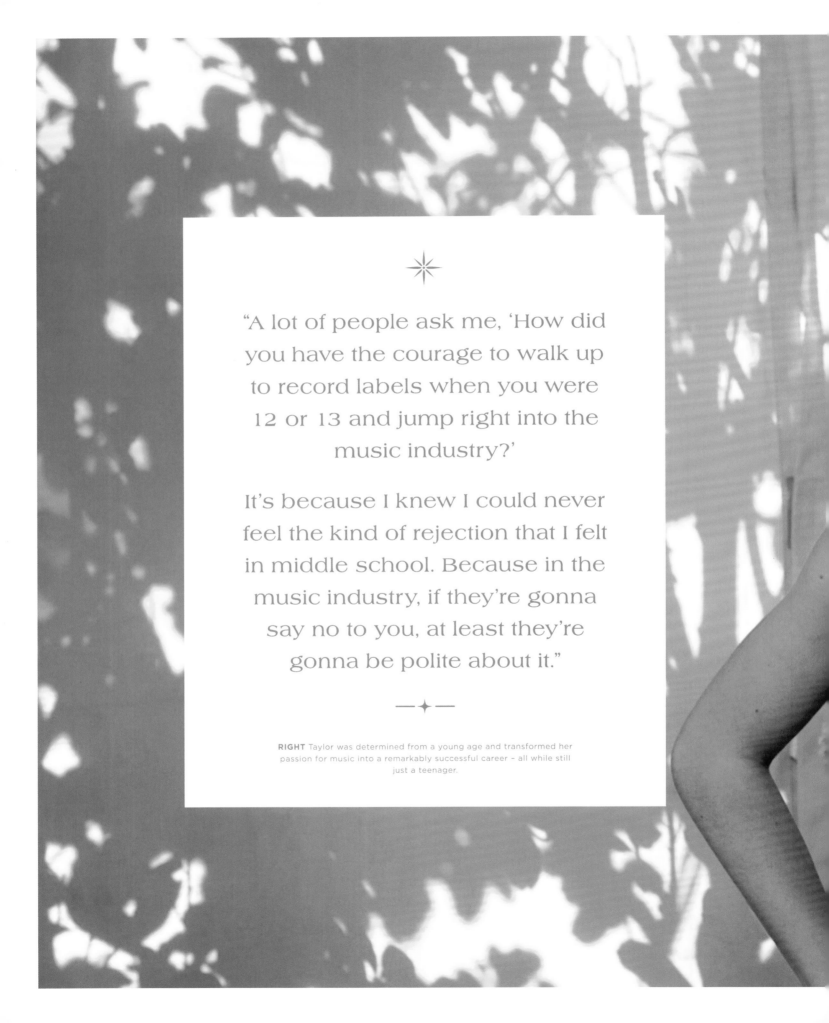

"A lot of people ask me, 'How did you have the courage to walk up to record labels when you were 12 or 13 and jump right into the music industry?'

It's because I knew I could never feel the kind of rejection that I felt in middle school. Because in the music industry, if they're gonna say no to you, at least they're gonna be polite about it."

RIGHT Taylor was determined from a young age and transformed her passion for music into a remarkably successful career – all while still just a teenager.

CHAPTER 2
THE EVOLUTION OF TAYLOR SWIFT

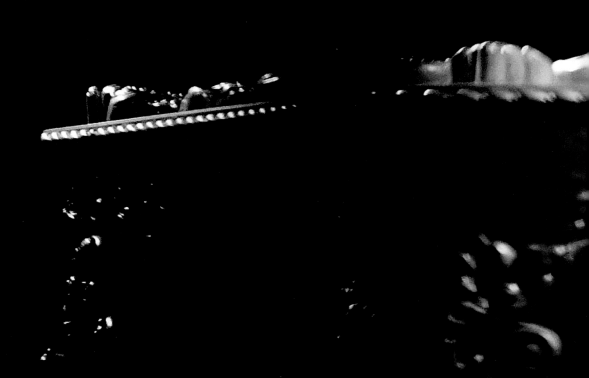

THE EVOLUTION OF TAYLOR SWIFT

The wide-eyed country starlet has transformed herself into a refined record-breaking artist by turning real life into marketable music

The 16-year-old girl that took the world by storm has certainly changed a lot throughout her remarkable career. Now a sophisticated, self-assured superstar, Taylor has evolved with every album, from her self-titled country debut, through the retro sounds of *1989*, to the dreamy electro-pop of *Midnights*. While she has been something of a genre-defying chameleon over the years – incorporating elements of everything from rock and electronica, to dubstep and hip hop in her tracks – Taylor's extraordinary songwriting talent has remained at the core of her music and appeal, and has played a major role in her success.

When she was starting out in Nashville, Taylor's songwriting is what made her stand out. After the family moved from Pennsylvania to Tennessee, Taylor spent as much time writing and performing as possible. She was offered a development deal with RCA Records and had signed a songwriter contract with Sony/ATV by the time she was still only 14. The following year, Taylor signed her first record deal with Big Machine Records. She would hurry to the studio after school, often bringing high school gossip to share with her writing partner, Liz Rose. Just like the country stars that influenced Taylor as a child, the pair worked Taylor's real-life experiences and emotions into the catchy songs that would make up her self-titled debut album, which was released on 24 October 2006.

The lyrics throughout *Taylor Swift* displayed her maturity and unbelievable talent. She was singing about typical teenage experiences – like driving pickup trucks and sneaking out late to meet her boyfriend – but also explored the themes of monogamy, heartbreak and infidelity. It was the first impression she made on the world and established her growing brand very well. She had yet to fully form her own style, but her songs were heartfelt with little flashes of comedy. She was on her way to becoming the recording artist we know and love today.

Once the album was out, Taylor's life changed dramatically. She hit the road and spent most of 2006 performing, promoting her album and touring with bigger country acts to raise her profile. Audiences loved her upbeat sound with her honest and relatable lyrics. Critics were impressed that so many of the songs were self-written, and she quickly became renowned for her ability to make heartfelt music that was also a commercial success. Industry professionals soon realised that she had found an untapped market in teenagers that listened to country music. Her track 'Our Song' made it to number one in the

LEFT Fifteen years of Taylor's red carpet glamour, from the 2009 Grammys, 2014 Met Gala and 2024 Golden Globes.

"Taylor was fulfilling lifelong dreams while she was still just a teenager"

country charts and Taylor began winning awards for both her writing and vocals.

The two years following her first album were filled with live performances, television appearances and making music videos for the singles on her first album. She was creating songs behind the scenes and learning a lot about the industry she had been launched into. By the time she was 18, Taylor's second album, *Fearless*, was ready to drop. While some more pop elements had crept onto the album, it maintained a similar sound to her first record – Taylor was still very much a country artist. She continued to wear cowboy boots to her events and performances and dressed in her trademark summer dresses and flowing gowns.

Fearless started to earn Taylor major awards. She became the youngest ever recipient of a Grammy for Album of the Year at the time, and the record became one of the best-selling albums of the 21st century so far. Taylor was already fulfilling lifelong dreams while still just a teenager. She was growing up and gaining confidence; her appeal was broadening and she was learning from her experiences. At this point she was already an established celebrity, but she continued working on songs that resonated with the typical teenage experience.

Taylor released her next album two months before her 21st birthday. *Speak Now* featured a subtle shift towards more diverse musical styles and began to stray from her staple theme of romantic relationships. It was the first album she wrote completely independently without any outside help. Taylor had compiled a bank of tracks that she had written solo over the years, adding new ones that she had penned late at night while on tour. The music was more mature and addressed topics like losing your youth, finding your own voice and dealing with criticism. *Speak Now* also notably featured Taylor's first apology to an ex in 'Back to December'. The album reflected her growth and maturity from her early successes as a young teen. As a pop album with sprinkles of country, it appealed to a wider audience and sold more than 1 million copies in the first week.

The release of *Red* in 2012 was a significant moment in Taylor's career. The album was a blend of pop, rock

and dubstep with elements of electronic and country. The themes in the lyrics were slightly edgier than her previous releases but the big hits stayed on message. 'I Knew You Were Trouble' and 'We Are Never Ever Getting Back Together' were both breakup anthems and '22' was a celebration of youth. She had made a name for herself in the industry at this point and was able to start collaborating with big names like Ed Sheeran. This was the period Taylor really switched up her look, too. Gone were the sun-kissed country curls and in came the dark blonde blunt bangs. This change of image stuck and became her new trademark, including red lipstick to match her chart-topping album.

By the time *1989* was released, Taylor had completed her transition from country singer to mainstream artist. Despite her astronomical success, being on the global stage meant the entire world was free to criticise her. She responded by using her songwriting superpower. 'Shake It Off' was the first single from her fifth album and it was a response to the unprovoked unpleasantries that had been directed at her. 'Blank Space' addressed the public perception of her dating life. She was under fire in the tabloids for having – what some people deemed – too many boyfriends, but releasing a song poking fun at the situation was her genius way to clap back. Taylor had reached the point where she was confident enough to own how she was being perceived in the media, and talented enough to be able to respond with a number one hit.

Taylor's high-profile feud with Kanye West reared its ugly head in 2016. After Taylor objected to being insulted in his song 'Famous', Kanye and his then wife Kim Kardashian released a recording that appeared to feature Taylor approving the idea. It was later revealed that the clip had been edited and manipulated to direct blame towards her. She experienced a backlash and withdrew from public

RIGHT A portrait from 2010. When *Speak Now* was released, Taylor was one of the biggest stars in music, and still only 20 years old.

Don Arnold/TAS18/Getty Images.

appearances for a year. She spoke about the experience of feeling hated by the whole planet in the 2020 documentary *Miss Americana*. Throughout her time behind closed doors, she evaluated what was truly important to her and started writing songs about what was in her heart.

Taylor stepped back into the spotlight with a new album called *reputation*. Her public image had taken a hit but she wasn't beaten by it. She used a major setback as an opportunity to shine light on the issue of artists facing unrelenting hate and feeling pressure to constantly reinvent themselves or be forgotten. Taylor made it clear that, despite Kanye West taking credit, she had earned her fame herself. She had worked incredibly hard to pursue music from a young age, and wanted the world to see she wasn't a woman that could be swept under the rug.

The driving force behind bringing big problems to the world's attention was the sexual assault she had been a victim of several years previously. In 2013 radio DJ David Mueller groped her after reaching up her skirt during a photo op. The case came to public attention in 2015 when the perpetrator of the assault filed defamation charges against Taylor for speaking up about it. She filed a countersuit and gave evidence in court. When the verdict ruled in Taylor's favour, Mueller lost both the case and his job. The ordeal highlighted the fact that the majority of

sexual assaults on women don't get reported, and many that do aren't taken seriously. It was after this event that she realised she had no choice but to use her platform to comment on world events and speak up for people that were being oppressed.

Before the release of her seventh album, Taylor had yet another obstacle to face. Many record deals require an artist to sign over all rights to their music. Taylor was no exception, and is not legally the owner of her first six albums. When the time came to renew her contract with Big Machine Records, she reportedly offered to pay for ownership during negotiations. The CEO, Scott Borchetta, refused because retaining the rights to her music made the company so valuable that he could sell it for a tidy profit. Accounts differ, but he is said to have offered her the chance to earn ownership, either by handing over even more music for the company's portfolio or by remaining in her contract for a further ten years. Taylor walked away from the deal

— ✦ —

ABOVE While she has experimented with different genres over the years, Taylor's distinctive songwriting hasn't changed.

LEFT Taylor's fashion has evolved alongside her music. *1989* was inspired by 80s pop, and Taylor's style followed suit.

"Taylor went from being teased, alone and unknown to a global superstar"

—✦—

and signed with a different label called Republic Records, on the condition that she would retain the rights to her work. *Lover*, released in August 2019, was the first album Taylor released that she owns outright. She wrote openly about the ordeal online to raise awareness of the issue of young artists being exploited for money.

Taylor's crusade to tackle big issues in song continued on *Lover*. The lead single – 'ME!' – advocated for self-confidence and individuality. Taylor wanted her young fans to sing along and belt out the lyrics to inspire them to love themselves for who they are.

'You Need to Calm Down' came next, showing Taylor's strong support for the LGBTQ+ community and harsh criticism for those that oppose and attempt to suppress queer culture. At the end of the accompanying music video, there was a message asking viewers to sign Taylor's Equality Act petition. If passed, the Equality Act will help ensure that all people are granted the same legal protections, regardless of their sexuality or gender.

'The Man' was *Lover*'s fourth single, calling out some of the ridiculous double-standards that women face every day of their lives. The song emphasised how the actions of women are scrutinised and interpreted differently than those of men, especially when it comes to their work and love lives. The wonderfully satirical video also saw Taylor transformed into 'Tyler Swift'.

Taylor's Lover Fest world tour was sadly cancelled due to the Covid-19 pandemic. Instead, she wrote, recorded and released two 'sister' albums in 2020's lockdowns – *folklore* and *evermore*. Taylor worked remotely with her long-time collaborator, Jack Antonoff, and The National's Aaron Dessner on both albums, leaving behind the upbeat pop of *Lover* to embrace a stripped-back, indie sound. Taylor also experimented with her songwriting style, creating wistful stories around a cast of fictional characters, rather than the more personal songs that fans had come to expect.

The records were a complete surprise to both fans and critics, and not only because Taylor announced their existence mere hours before each release. The low-fi sound and Taylor's evolved songwriting style were quite different to any of her previous albums, but many music critics regard them as the best albums of her career so far.

In October 2022, Taylor returned to pop with her tenth studio album *Midnights*, but this was not the same flavour of pop as *1989* or *Lover*. A concept album inspired by her "sleepless nights", this record explored Taylor's anxieties and insecurities with confessional lyrics set to dreamy, electro-pop beats. It became the best-selling album of 2022, and critics praised her (sometimes brutal) honesty and self-reflection. It was arguably Taylor's most mature album to date, with moments of darkness such as lead single 'Anti-Hero', which she described as "a real guided tour throughout all of the things I tend to hate about myself". It's also one of her favourite songs she's ever written, as she explained "because I think it's really honest".

When Taylor announced her first tour in five years, it wasn't only going to encompass the four albums she had released since *reputation*, it was going to include her entire back catalogue. The Eras Tour is a celebration of her extraordinary evolution – an ambitious show packed with highlights from her first ten albums. Eras has become a global phenomenon in its own right; it's a record-breaking showcase of Taylor's truly remarkable career.

At the time of writing, the next step in Taylor's evolution is coming very soon indeed. At the Grammys in February 2024, she announced that her 11th studio album, *The Tortured Poets Department*, would be released in April.

Taylor has come a long way from being a little kid obsessed with singing to a respected musician and cultural icon willing to take risks to do what she believes is right. She went from being teased, alone and unknown to a superstar with millions of fans all around the world. Even though she's been writing and performing for nearly two decades, Taylor isn't slowing down and will continue to inspire people for years to come.

—✦—

RIGHT The Eras Tour takes fans on a journey through Taylor's entire musical evolution so far.

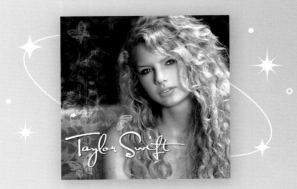

TAYLOR SWIFT

Released when she was just 16, Taylor wrote many of the songs
for her debut album while in her first year of high school

RELEASE DATE 24 OCTOBER 2006

TIM MCGRAW

The idea for this song came to Taylor when she was in
maths class during her freshman year of high school. Her
senior boyfriend was due to graduate and move away to
college at the end of the academic year. Writing this track
helped her deal with her sadness. She wanted to capture
the bittersweet nature of a painful breakup and the happy
memories that go on long after the relationship is over.
The title 'Tim McGraw' is about Taylor's love of the
country icon and how his music will always remind her
of her first high school romance. Taylor took her concept
to country music writer Liz Rose and the pair finished the
song in just 20 minutes.

PICTURE TO BURN

Taylor herself described the second track on the album
as brutally honest. It was about a high school fling that
was never 'official'. Taylor became frustrated by the boy's
arrogance and selfishness. She ranted about him, shouting
"I hate his stupid truck that he doesn't let me drive! He's
such a redneck!" This outburst became the building
blocks for the chorus and gave the song its comical edge.
'Picture to Burn' was released as a single after it got
enthusiastic reactions from the audience while Taylor was
on tour supporting Rascal Flatts.

TEARDROPS ON MY GUITAR

This song was inspired by Taylor's unrequited feelings for a
boy at school named Drew. He only saw her as a friend, but
they sat together in classes and became very close. Soon he
began to open up about another girl he liked and Taylor
nodded along and supported him while her heart was
breaking. She endured the torture of watching the pair date
for several years and never told him how she felt. When the
song was released he tried to make contact with Taylor but
she felt too awkward to respond to any of his messages.

A PLACE IN THIS WORLD

Taylor wrote this song at 13 when she had just moved to
Nashville to pursue music. She'd forgotten she had written
it, but found it again when putting the album together.
Taylor decided to include it because it was about pursuing
her dreams as an artist, and this album was the first step
towards achieving them. She considered naming the album
after this song, but eventually went with her own name to
help her get recognition.

RIGHT Taylor at the CMA Music Festival in June 2007, where she
played 'Tim McGraw' from her debut.

"'Cold as You' began Taylor's tradition of putting her most emotionally raw songs as the fifth track on each of her albums"

COLD AS YOU

This is Taylor's favourite song on this entire album. She was interested in a boy who wasn't emotionally available and had endured just about enough. The song is about the moment she realised he wasn't who she had thought he was. She regretted making excuses for him and realised she was wasting her time being in that relationship. Taylor was very pleased with the honest and vulnerable nature of lyrics that she and writing partner Liz Rose put together. This began Taylor's tradition of putting her most emotionally raw songs as the fifth track on each of her albums.

THE OUTSIDE

Taylor wrote this ballad about loneliness when she was only 12. She felt like an outcast at school and used music as an escape. She was taller than all the other girls and was obsessed with country music, while everyone else was going to parties and sleepovers. She would wake up in the morning not knowing if anybody at school would talk to her or if she was about to face another day of isolation. Looking back on this period of her life, Taylor says she's thankful she wasn't one of the 'cool kids' or she might never have found music.

TIED TOGETHER WITH A SMILE

Despite still being relatively young, Taylor found she could observe other people going through struggles and produce incredibly insightful and empathetic songs based on what she saw. This particular track is about one of her friends who was popular in high school and performed in beauty pageants. All the girls at school were jealous of her, and all the boys were interested in her. While she seemed to have a perfect life, this girl developed an eating disorder. Taylor wrote this song the day she found out about her friend's condition, having been struck by how easy it is to hide such deep pain behind a smile.

STAY BEAUTIFUL

Other country artists admired Taylor for having the guts to name real people in her music. 'Stay Beautiful' is about a boy called Cory who Taylor had a crush on, but the two never got together. She has stated emphatically that a lot of her romantic songs are based on observation rather than her personal experience. Taylor revealed that she barely even spoke to him, but was inspired to write a song just from watching him. Alas it wasn't meant to be – Cory moved away before anything could happen between them, and she sang this song at the school talent show after he was gone.

Words by Amy Grisdale. Image: Tony R. Phipps/WireImage/Getty Images.

SHOULD'VE SAID NO

The fifth and final single of this album went platinum and topped the country charts. It's about being cheated on in a relationship where everything else was going so well. This exact thing happened to Taylor when she was 16, and the title of the track popped into her head immediately after she discovered the news. The chorus was finished in five minutes flat, and she used some of what she actually said to her boyfriend as they broke up in real life. Taylor gave a very memorable performance of this track at the 2008 Academy of Country Music Awards.

MARY'S SONG (OH MY MY MY)

In a world full of tabloid reports of high-profile breakups and infidelity, Taylor decided to take inspiration from the elderly couple that lived next door to her family. The pair had met as children and fell in love as they grew up. They had been married a long time and Taylor was struck by how all she needed to see a good example of 'forever love' was to go home. The song she wrote in response is about how sometimes love can be everlasting even if others don't believe it.

OUR SONG

As a resourceful young girl, when Taylor didn't have 'a song' with her high school boyfriend, she wrote one herself. Like 'Tim McGraw', it took her just 20 minutes to write the track. She performed it at a freshman talent show in high school, and found that her classmates could recite large sections after only hearing it once. 'Our Song' was very well received when she released it as a record, earning her several country music awards. It was hard for critics to believe a girl so young could use mature themes and tell such a compelling story.

LEFT Taylor pictured at the 42nd Annual Academy of Country Music Awards with two of her idols, Faith Hill and Tim McGraw (who she named her debut single after).

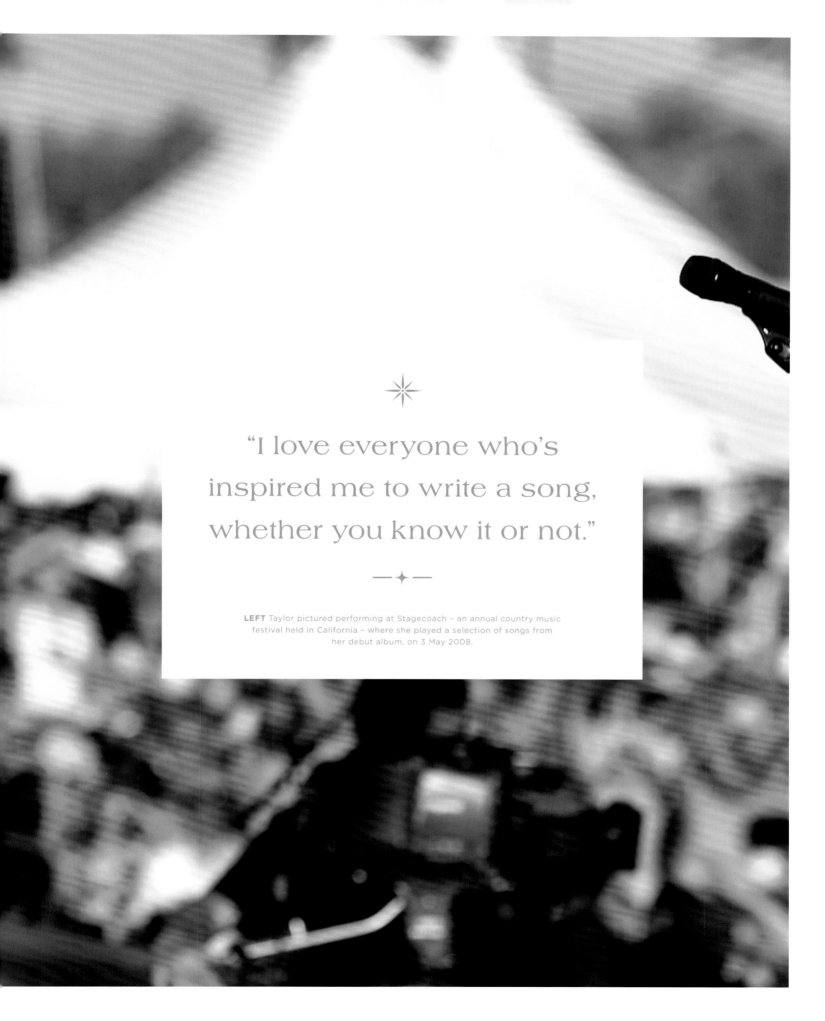

"I love everyone who's inspired me to write a song, whether you know it or not."

LEFT Taylor pictured performing at Stagecoach – an annual country music festival held in California – where she played a selection of songs from her debut album, on 3 May 2008.

FEARLESS

After creating this seamless blend of country and pop, Taylor became the youngest winner of an Album of the Year Grammy

RELEASE DATE 11 NOVEMBER 2008

FEARLESS

By the time Taylor started writing this album, she was busy touring and opening for other musical acts. She wasn't remotely close to getting into another relationship but wanted to write about the fearlessness of falling in love, regardless of the prospect of getting hurt once again. "[Sometimes] you write about what you wish you had," she explained, "So, this song is about the best first date I haven't had yet." In the album's liner notes, Taylor explains that her personal definition of 'fearless' isn't about being invincible. It's about acknowledging your fears but taking the risk anyway. She was so in love with the concept that she named her album after it.

FIFTEEN

The subject of this song is Taylor's best friend, Abigail Anderson. It tells the story of their first year in high school together, which was the year Taylor really started to notice that she was growing up. She wanted to pen a cautionary tale including all the things she wished she had known when she was that age. She and Abigail both had their hearts broken during freshman year. Taylor cried when recording the track because the pain of her close friend resonated so deeply with her. The song makes her emotional to this day.

LOVE STORY

Influenced by *Romeo and Juliet*, this track tells the story of a forbidden romance, but thankfully the song has a much happier ending than Shakespeare's tragic play. She wrote it on the floor of her bedroom, not wanting to stop because she felt so inspired. This was Taylor's first global hit, becoming one of the best-selling singles of all time. Critics gushed about the passionate and heart-warming nature of the song, as well as the catchy tune that fans couldn't resist singing along to.

HEY STEPHEN

A young man who opened a few shows for Taylor caught her eye. She was too shy to say something so she put it in a song instead. The lyrics talk about Taylor imagining the pair in romantic scenarios and wishing he would take notice of her, even though she knows it probably won't go anywhere. She reportedly sent him a text after the album was released telling him to check out track four. His reply was long and he was excited, but they never got together.

RIGHT Taylor embarked on her first headline tour in support of this album, playing over 100 shows between April 2009 and July 2010.

WHITE HORSE

Taylor wrote this track about what she says was the worst part of a breakup with someone she thought was her Prince Charming. It's that moment she realised that all of the dreams and future plans she had for the relationship were gone forever in an instant. She thought the track was a little too solemn for *Fearless* and planned to save it for her third album, until she was given an offer she couldn't refuse. The producers of one of her favourite TV shows, *Grey's Anatomy*, heard the song and asked to use it in the series. 'White Horse' went on to feature in the first episode of the fifth season and made it onto her second album.

YOU BELONG WITH ME

Taylor had the idea for this one when she overheard one of her male friends trying to soothe his angry girlfriend over the phone. She felt sorry for him and came up with the idea of a girl-next-door character that the love interest always overlooks. She plays both girls in the video alongside actor Lucas Till, who appeared in *Hannah Montana: The Movie* with Taylor the same year. The video raked in millions of views and won the Best Female Video VMA in 2009. Her victory was overshadowed by media coverage after Kanye West stormed the stage to say that he thought Beyoncé should have won the award instead.

BREATHE (FEAT. COLBIE CAILLAT)

Co-written with singer-songwriter Colbie Caillat, 'Breathe' is about the ending of a friendship. Taylor and Colbie decided to keep the lyrics open to interpretation so that more fans could identify with the song in their own way. It was nominated for a Grammy for Best Pop Collaboration, but the award went to 'Lucky' by Jason Mraz and – coincidentally – Colbie Caillat. Initially, Colbie was just going to sing the backing vocals on 'Breathe', but Taylor liked her work so much that she included her far more than originally planned throughout the song. Taylor wanted to make sure Colbie was featured enough that fans could recognise her voice immediately.

TELL ME WHY

On the day this track was composed, Taylor went to the house of her writing partner, Liz Rose, and ranted about her relationship. Together they worked her rambling speech into a song about a girl getting sick and tired of her boyfriend hurting her feelings. It paints a picture of a boyfriend with a bad temper that constantly blows hot and cold. The man in question was not named in the song, but fans speculate that it was about singer Joe Jonas. He and Taylor were together for a brief period in 2008 and unfortunately the relationship ended sourly.

YOU'RE NOT SORRY

Taylor writes music as an emotional outlet. She created this track when she had reached what she described as 'breaking point' after she had found out about a number of troubling secrets about her boyfriend. This series of discoveries was alarming enough to prompt the end of the relationship, as Taylor didn't want to let him hurt her any longer. The remixed single was re-released in March 2009 on the same day Taylor had a cameo role in the 16th episode of *CSI: Crime Scene Investigation* season nine.

THE WAY I LOVED YOU

There are a lot of things that can go wrong in a relationship, especially when the couple is young and uncertain about the future. This song is inspired by the time Taylor realised that the relationship she was in was 'too perfect' and she wanted something more. She missed being so in love that it made her crazy and described the feeling as a rollercoaster rush. The lyrics talk about how they can never go back to how things used to be after this epiphany, and sometimes two people just aren't right for each other even though they may seem very compatible on paper.

FOREVER & ALWAYS

Though he's not named in the song, it's widely accepted that this track is about Joe Jonas. Taylor was a guest on *Ellen* in November 2008 and told the host that this song was a last-minute addition to the album. She had been through a hard breakup that occurred during a 25 second phone call. The song talks about the feeling of being under the same storm cloud when they were together and when she was alone. In another appearance on *Ellen* ten years later, Taylor apologised to Joe for the savage lyrics.

THE BEST DAY

This song was a Christmas present to her mother, Andrea Swift. They are extremely close and Andrea usually tours the world with her daughter. Taylor wrote this track when they were on the road and recorded it in secret. She then made a compilation of home videos, which went on to become the official music video. She played it on Christmas day and Andrea burst into tears when she realised Taylor had arranged such a touching surprise for her.

CHANGE

Taylor wrote this the morning after winning a Country Music Horizon Award in 2009. She was part of a small record label in an industry full of fierce competition. She was gaining popularity and recognition even though she was still in high school. 'Change' is about a turning of the tide towards victory from what seemed like inevitable defeat. Her songs usually contain hidden details and messages for her fervent fans. The secret meaning of this song is Taylor's gratitude that the fans were what made things change for her.

— ✦ —

RIGHT *Fearless* earned Taylor a haul of trophies at the 52nd Grammy Awards in 2010, including the coveted Album of the Year honour.

"To me, 'fearless' is not the absence of fear. It's not being completely unafraid.

To me, fearless is having fears. Fearless is having doubts. Lots of them. To me, fearless is living in spite of those things that scare you to death."

—✦—

LEFT Taylor in her 'You Belong with Me' marching band outfit during the Fearless Tour show at New York City's Madison Square Garden, on 27 August 2009.

SPEAK NOW

Every single released from this record went either platinum or multi-platinum, and Taylor wrote the entire album single-handedly

RELEASE DATE 25 OCTOBER 2010

MINE

An internet leak meant fans got to listen to this single two weeks early, forcing it to be sent out to radio stations ahead of schedule. It was the first single released from Taylor's highly anticipated album, reaching number two in the charts and winning four of the 12 awards it was nominated for. Taylor knew the song would be a hit after recording a demo with producer Nathan Chapman in one day. The pair had a moment where they both were overcome with the feeling that 'Mine' was the song to lead the charge.

SPARKS FLY

This was written back when Taylor was 16. She had performed it live at a California casino in 2007, where it was played on the banjo accompanied by violins, and had slightly different lyrics to the album version. Videos of the show were put online, and fans requested that she officially release the song – so she did. She'd been working on the song for years, and enjoyed seeing it develop to the point where it was ready to be heard.

RIGHT *Speak Now* was an examination of Taylor's journey into adulthood, and was more reflective than her first two albums.

BACK TO DECEMBER

Taylor has admitted that this was the first time she had apologised in a song. In a 2016 Facebook Live stream, her ex-boyfriend, the *Twilight* actor Taylor Lautner, confirmed fans' suspicions that 'Back to December' was indeed about him. The two Taylors – affectionately nicknamed Taylor Squared – were both cast in the 2010 rom-com *Valentine's Day* and were seen together at hockey games for several months after filming had wrapped in 2009. They broke up in December that year, a month before the film came out in cinemas. The song is a message to a sweet and respectful boy, expressing gratitude for the relationship and sincere regret over how she ended things.

SPEAK NOW

Before a marriage takes place the officiant asks if anybody present knows of any reason why the wedding shouldn't go ahead. The congregation are told to "Speak now or forever hold your peace". Taylor had the idea for this track when she was listening to a friend complaining that her ex-boyfriend was about to marry a 'mean' girl. Taylor asked her out of the blue, "So, you gonna speak now?" and joked about storming the wedding with her guitar. She reflected later about how hurtful it must be to watch somebody you love marry somebody else, and wrote this song.

"Taylor saw herself in the faces in the crowds at her performances and wanted to tell young fans not to wish their childhoods away"

DEAR JOHN

The subject of this song is suspected to be singer-songwriter John Mayer, who Taylor dated for a few months after the pair recorded the duet, 'Half of My Heart' together for his 2009 album *Battle Studies*. The song explores her frustrations with the relationship: "You are an expert at sorry and keeping lines blurry [...] Don't you think I was too young to be messed with?" Mayer dismissed it as 'cheap' songwriting. In response, Taylor said in an interview with *Glamour* that it was 'presumptuous' of Mayer to assume the song was about him.

MEAN

It's rumoured that this was written about blogger Bob Lefsetz who wrote scathing reviews of Taylor's music and live performances. He also had highly publicised feuds with Kid Rock and Kiss icon Gene Simmons. Taylor wanted to point out that there's a difference between giving an artist constructive criticism and being downright mean. She felt that certain people were crossing the line repeatedly and attacking everything she did. Writing this song helped Taylor deal with the fact that no matter where you go in life some people are going to be mean to you.

THE STORY OF US

Running into an ex can be awkward, especially if you get seated a few feet away from each other at the CMT Awards. This is exactly what happened to Taylor and John Mayer. She described the experience as a silent war, where each person was trying to show how little they cared that the other was there. She was ignoring him and talking to people she didn't know, even though there was a person she had a lot to say to just six chairs away. It made her feel like she was alone in a crowded room, so she crafted this song around the frustration she felt in a situation she found "terribly, heartbreakingly awkward".

NEVER GROW UP

Taylor had mixed feelings about growing up, which isn't surprising as she did it under the scrutiny of the public eye. As a child she had longed to be older but, looking back, she realised she should have enjoyed being a little kid as long as she could. She wrote this song as a message to her young fans. She saw herself in the faces in the crowds at her performances and wanted to tell them not to wish their childhoods away. In 2015, she dedicated a performance of the track to her godson, Leo Thames (son of model and actress Jaime King), explaining that his birth had given the song a whole new meaning to her.

Words by Amy Grisdale. Image: Kevin Mazur/WireImage/Getty Images.

"Taylor has said that 'Long Live' is a love song written to the team behind her"

ENCHANTED

Once again Taylor was able to channel her emotional intelligence and maturity into music. She met Adam Young (of Owl City) after exchanging some phone calls and emails, and they got on well. She wrote the lyrics for this song after Adam emailed to say he was 'wonderstruck' to meet her. After the song was released Adam recorded his own version of it and sent it to Taylor with a note that called her a modern-day Cinderella and that he was enchanted to meet her too. Taylor considered naming the album after this track, before settling on *Speak Now*.

BETTER THAN REVENGE

Deviating from country-pop, this track was influenced by pop-punk, telling the story of a girl who Taylor said stole her boyfriend. She felt compelled to create a track inspired by the idea of revenge, but the song was criticised for its harsher 'anti-feminist' lyrics (which she changed in the 2023 Taylor's Version release). In a 2014 interview with *The Guardian*, Taylor reflected on the song and said she now knows that partners can't be stolen from you if they don't want to leave.

INNOCENT

Taylor described 'Innocent' as an open letter to somebody she forgave in front of the whole world. That statement, coupled with a few clues in the lyrics, suggested it's about Kanye West: "32, and still growing up now" (Kanye was 32 at the time of the 2009 VMAs). She thought it was only right to put it on this album. *Speak Now* is about figuring out how you feel and saying something about it. Some critics called it passive-aggressive while others called it beautiful. She performed this track for the very first time at the VMAs in 2010, one year after the Kanye West incident.

HAUNTED

Sometimes in a relationship, one person starts to drift away and the love begins to fade. Taylor was going through this exact situation when she woke up in the middle of the night ready to write a song. Once she had the words she knew she needed to make the song a big production to reflect its intensity. She recruited award-winning cellist and conductor Paul Buckmaster to add a string section to the track. Buckmaster had collaborated with legendary artists throughout his career, from Celine Dion to David Bowie.

LAST KISS

Once again, Taylor used her life experience to pen this track. She was struck by the feelings of anger, frustration and confusion after a breakup and the utter sadness all of those feelings settle into. Rumour has it that 'Last Kiss' was written about Joe Jonas, but – true to form – Taylor has neither confirmed nor denied this suspicion. The lyrics describe her reflections on the relationship, looking back on the good times that she didn't think would ever come to an end. She admits to herself that there were a lot of emotions, hopes and memories she missed experiencing when she was in love.

LONG LIVE

The last song of the album is an anthem of victory. It's about all the moments of triumph and celebration of the first few years of her career. Taylor says it was a love song dedicated to the team behind her. She wrote every single track on the album by herself, but had a whole crew of people helping with its production and release, as well as the support from her millions of fans. She says all these people helped build her as an artist brick by brick and she wanted to share her success with them all.

LEFT Taylor pictured backstage with Speak Now World Tour special guests Selena Gomez and James Taylor (who she was named after). Taylor sang 'Who Says' with Selena and 'Fire and Rain' with James.

"I think most of us fear reaching the end of our life, and looking back regretting the moments we didn't speak up.

When we didn't say 'I love you.' When we should've said 'I'm sorry.' When we didn't stand up for ourselves or someone who needed help.

These songs are made up of words I didn't say when the moment was right in front of me."

RIGHT Taylor on stage in Rotterdam during the Speak Now World Tour. Between 2011 and 2012, she played 110 shows in 19 countries spanning four continents.

RED

Stepping further from her country roots, Taylor's fourth album featured superstar collaborations and varied musical styles

RELEASE DATE 22 OCTOBER 2012

STATE OF GRACE

The opening track of this album was released as the fourth single. Critics praised *Red*'s broad style as almost all of her previous music had a lot of country influence. Taylor went on *Good Morning America* in October 2012 to give the world a sneak preview of this track. On the show she said the song was about the endless possibilities before you when you first fall in love. Viewers only heard a snippet of the chorus and had to wait more than a week for the 16-track album to come out in full.

RED

Taylor uses colours to express her different emotions throughout this song. She explained that the two years leading up to this album were full of crazy and tumultuous feelings, and she was inspired by that intensity. She sang about blue representing the feeling of losing a lover, while missing him seemed dark grey. Red was what she felt when she loved him. Critics praised the lyrics' honesty and heart, as well as the musicality and production of the song.

RIGHT Taylor performing 'We Are Never Ever Getting Back Together' at the MTV EMAs in 2012, in her iconic ringmaster outfit.

22

Despite massive success in songwriting and performing, Taylor sometimes found critics still dismissed her music because of her youth. This track flaunted her youth in the face of her older critics with a new bubblegum pop sound. She has stated in interviews that being 22 taught her a lot about letting loose in the face of fear and indecision. She said it's an age where you are aware that you don't have very much life experience, and that there are a lot of life lessons ahead. This is the time to enjoy being carefree, even if it's only for a short while.

I ALMOST DO

Going back to her Nashville roots with a heavy country feel, 'I Almost Do' expresses Taylor's feelings of missing a former partner. She explained in an interview with *USA Today* that when the relationship this song is about ended, she was so crushed that she suffered six months of writer's block before starting to create this album. The lyrics discuss loneliness and a near-irresistible urge to pick up the phone and talk to him: "I just want to tell you, it takes everything in me not to call you […] Every time I don't, I almost do". She wonders if he's thinking about her and says that even though their relationship was messy, she still dreams about it and almost wishes they were still together.

ALL TOO WELL

Taylor said this track was the most difficult to compose on the whole album. It began with her playing the chords over and over and ranting about the hardship she was experiencing. She had to filter the elements down or she would have ended up with a much longer song that – she assumed – nobody would have listened to (how wrong she was!) She recruited long-time writing partner Liz Rose to help prune away the less important parts. Even with two expert writers chopping it down it still came out as the longest track on the album at five minutes and 28 seconds.

TREACHEROUS

This track is about a relationship in Taylor's life that she knew would end badly. She said it had a magnetic draw that didn't allow her to escape the heartbreak. The song received huge critical acclaim for maintaining the high standard of quality in the previous album, *Speak Now*. The verses were praised for their 'hushed, confessional beauty' and critics wrote that Taylor's vocals were going from strength to strength. Taylor collaborated with Dan Wilson of the band Semisonic, who had previously worked with Adele on her hit song 'Someone Like You'.

I KNEW YOU WERE TROUBLE

This was one of Taylor's favourite songs on the entire album because it reflects the chaos she felt when writing it. People speculate that it was written about John Mayer, but Taylor has declined to comment on the subject of the song. She composed it on her own and the media loved its mainstream appeal with the added touch of dubstep in the chorus. It became her 14th top 10 hit and made Taylor the first artist in digital history to debut two songs with more than 400,000 sales. It earned her another VMA for Best Female Video and won another four awards of the nine for which it was nominated.

WE ARE NEVER EVER GETTING BACK TOGETHER

This breakup anthem was the first single to be released from *Red* and topped the charts around the world. Having written her previous album solo she was keen to work with other artists again. She invited two Swedish musicians, Max Martin and Shellback, to collaborate on a new track. Taylor had heard rumours from a friend that she was getting back together with an old flame. Max and Shellback asked for the details, so Taylor told them about their dynamic of splitting up and reuniting, and the lyrics flowed naturally from there.

STAY STAY STAY

As the title suggests, this one is about pleading with a lover to remain in the relationship with her. The press criticised her for putting out so many songs about love and heartbreak in a short time. Taylor's songs are popular because they are full of her honest emotions and *Red* is about the rollercoaster ride she felt she was on throughout writing the album. The writing itself was draining as she had to hop from emotional lows when writing more mournful tracks to singing about how amazing it is to meet somebody new.

Words by Amy Grisdale. Image: Dave J Hogan/MTV/Getty Images.

"Ed Sheeran claims that when they disagreed over a chord, he bowed to Taylor's superior knowledge"

THE LAST TIME (FEAT. GARY LIGHTBODY)

Snow Patrol singer Gary Lightbody joined in with the writing and performance of the final single from *Red*. The alternative rock duet was produced by Jacknife Lee who is famous for working with bands like Snow Patrol and U2. The lyrics tell the story of a long-term relationship that is crumbling away piece by piece, with Swift's character granting Lightbody's character one final chance to salvage things between them. It was dubbed the most mature track on the album by critics.

HOLY GROUND

The lyrics of this track describe a difficult relationship that ended quickly, but the two are on good terms now. It's believed to be about Joe Jonas, but we don't know for sure. The song says that they had a brief period of perfection together before the couple split up, and in those good times everywhere they stepped together was 'holy ground'.

SAD BEAUTIFUL TRAGIC

This doesn't seem to be about one particular person, but fans have assumed it could have been inspired by either Taylor Lautner or Jake Gyllenhaal. Taylor wrote it sitting in her tour bus after a live show when she found herself thinking about an old relationship. She realised she wasn't sad or angry any more but felt a distinct wistful loss. She wanted the song to be a little bit ambiguous to mirror the murkiness of her memories of her past relationship. Taylor wanted her album to be all over the place like her feelings.

THE LUCKY ONE

Here, Taylor addresses her fears of falling into obscurity. The lyrics talk about a star who has everything, but cannot handle the pressure of constant media attention. There's speculation about who inspired this track, but it could be Kim Wilde. Taylor samples her song 'Four Letter Word' in 'The Lucky One' and refers to giving up performing to work in a rose garden (Kim Wilde left the spotlight and became a gardener). The song ends with Taylor saying that she understands why the star chose that path.

EVERYTHING HAS CHANGED (FEAT. ED SHEERAN)

Rumours were flying about Ed Sheeran appearing on this album for months before its release. They wrote this song together sitting out in Taylor's back garden and worked well as a team. Ed claims that when they disagreed over a chord, he bowed to Taylor's superior knowledge. The core concept of the song is how everything can seem completely different when you enter a new relationship. She says the impact of that particular person coming into your life is powerful and exciting and in the song she's eager to get to know them better.

STARLIGHT

Taylor came across an old photo of human rights advocate Ethel Kennedy and her husband Robert 'Bobby' F Kennedy. The photo was of the pair dancing at the age of 17 back in the 1940s. Taylor was so inspired by it that she decided to write a song about their relationship despite not knowing exactly how they got together. A few weeks later she bumped into one of Ethel and Robert's 11 children and had the chance to meet Ethel in person. Tragically Robert, like his brother John F Kennedy, was assassinated in the 1960s.

BEGIN AGAIN

Because so much of the album deviated from Taylor's traditional style, it's only right that *Red* ends with a country ballad. Taylor sings about a girl braving a first date with a new man after getting over a bad relationship. A girl in that situation can feel so vulnerable and the song encourages girls to be bold. In the song she talks about having things in common with the new man, including the music of James Taylor (after whom Taylor was named): "You said you never met one girl who had as many James Taylor records as you, but I do."

RIGHT 'Everything Has Changed' was the first song Taylor and Ed duetted on, but it wouldn't be the last.

"My experiences in love have taught me difficult lessons, especially my experiences with crazy love. The red relationships."

— ✦ —

RIGHT Taylor on stage at the Z100's Jingle Ball at Madison Square Garden in December 2012. She embarked on The Red Tour between 2013-14, performing the album to over 1.7 million fans around the world.

Taylor Swift   1989

1989

After flirting with pop on *Red*, Taylor moved away from country music altogether and established herself as a fully fledged pop star

RELEASE DATE 27 OCTOBER 2014

WELCOME TO NEW YORK

The album's opening track celebrates the endless possibilities available to people in New York City, where Taylor moved in 2014. She wrote the song with Ryan Tedder from OneRepublic, and wanted it to be the first track on the album because her relocation had such a big impact on her life around that time. The lyrics: "And you can want who you want, boys and boys and girls and girls" was interpreted as Taylor's shout out in support of the LGBTQ+ community.

BLANK SPACE

On the album's second single, Taylor pokes fun at the media's perception of her and her relationship history, with lyrics such as "Got a long list of ex-lovers, they'll tell you I'm insane." She creates a character that is an exaggeration of the man-eater she was portrayed to be in the media at that time. The electro-pop track was another collaboration with Swedish pop music extraordinaires Max Martin and Shellback, who contributed to many songs on this album.

RIGHT Taylor pictured during The 1989 World Tour in Tokyo, Japan, in May 2015. The show became the highest-grossing tour of that year.

STYLE

This is one of Taylor's more ambiguous tracks. While it may seem like a song about timeless style and fashion, with references to 1950s movie star James Dean and a classic red lip, the lyrics actually depict an unhealthy on-off relationship. Taylor sings about knowing they should finally call it quits yet they can't help crawling back to each other. Many fans interpreted the song to be about her ex-boyfriend Harry Styles – who is thought to have inspired several tracks on this album – thanks to the lyrics: "You've got that long hair, slicked back, white T-shirt."

OUT OF THE WOODS

On the sixth single off *1989*, Taylor looks back at a fragile, unstable relationship. The track contains the extremely specific lyrics: "Remember when you hit the brakes too soon, 20 stitches in a hospital room," a reference to a snowmobile accident she was involved in with an ex-boyfriend which nobody knew about until the song was released. It is widely believed that the ex in question is Styles, as he was pictured in December 2012, around the time they dated, with an injury to his chin. The lyrics "Your necklace hanging round my neck […] Two paper airplanes flying," also seem to be a reference to the matching necklaces they once wore.

ALL YOU HAD TO DO WAS STAY

In this song, Taylor sings directly to an ex who has reappeared after ending their relationship, and she has no interest in taking him back. She recalls how he shut her out and "drove us off the road" and firmly tells him he's too late and she's done with him, singing: "People like me are gone forever when you say goodbye." The track also features the recurring high-pitched yell "Stay!" throughout, which was inspired by a dream she had about an ex showing up at her door and that's the only sound that would come out of her mouth. This entry also follows Taylor's tradition of making the fifth song on her albums the most emotional.

SHAKE IT OFF

'Shake It Off' was the lead single from *1989* and made the clear statement that Taylor was now a full-on pop star. The uptempo dance-pop track, written with Martin and Shellback, addresses the rumours and misconceptions about her life and how she brushes them off and pays no attention to them so she can enjoy herself. The opening verse references the media portrayal of Taylor as a 'serial dater' ("I go on too many dates, but I can't make them stay, at least that's what people say.") While she makes light of it in the song, Taylor has often spoken about her frustrations with the media's obsession with her love life.

I WISH YOU WOULD

This song opens with a guy driving down a street in the middle of the night and he passes his ex-girlfriend's house. He assumes she hates him when she's actually still in love with him. Taylor directly addresses the ex and wishes she could go back in time and handle their rough patches differently, with lyrics like, "Wish I'd never hung up the phone like I did," and "I wish you knew that I'd never forget you as long as I live." She wrote the lyrics to a track Jack Antonoff had created, in a similar fashion to 'Out of the Woods'.

BAD BLOOD

The context of this song is probably the most well-known from *1989*, exploring Taylor's feud with Katy Perry. The song describes a betrayal by a close friend, and Taylor later clarified that it was about a female musician who tried to sabotage one of her tours by hiring some of her dancers. Although she didn't point fingers, it was quickly reported that Taylor was singing about losing her friendship with the 'Firework' singer. Their feud rumbled on for many years, but they finally buried the hatchet in 2018. A remixed version of the track – featuring a reworked instrumental and vocals by Kendrick Lamar on the verses – was released as the fourth single off *1989* and was accompanied by a star-studded music video.

WILDEST DREAMS

Slower than most of the songs on *1989*, the album's fifth single has a sultry, dream-like quality that sparked comparisons to Lana Del Rey's work. In the track, Taylor hopes that her lover will always remember her and the good memories they shared once they are over, and while she hopes it lasts, she knows it won't, with her singing: "I can see the ends as it begins" and "Someday when you leave me, I'd bet these memories follow you around."

Words by Hannah Wales. Image: Jun Sato/Getty Images.

HOW YOU GET THE GIRL

In this upbeat pop track, Taylor offers advice to a guy to help him win his ex back after he broke her heart by leaving without explanation six months before. She suggests ways to get back into the girl's good books and offers up recommendations of what to say. By the end of the song, Taylor's advice has been successful and the guy and girl in question are back together.

THIS LOVE

This slow and soft ballad is the only *1989* track written solely by Taylor. It also marks her reunion with Nathan Chapman, who produced many songs on her country-era albums. With her breathy, relaxing vocals, Taylor sings about the cyclical nature of a relationship – the good and the bad parts of it – and how a lover comes in and out of her life. The chorus began as a short poem Taylor wrote in her journal following a real-life event; she immediately heard the melody and knew it had to be a song.

I KNOW PLACES

In this track, Taylor sings about the effect fame has on a relationship and how difficult it is for a high-profile couple to maintain a private life. She uses a metaphor of a fox hunt, where they are the foxes and the media are the hunters, and speaks to a new lover to reassure them that she knows where they can go without anyone noticing. Taylor had the melody and majority of the lyrics down before a studio session with Tedder, and they completed and recorded it the following day.

CLEAN

Taylor created this emotional ballad with Imogen Heap, who co-wrote the track, played the instruments and sang background vocals. The song focuses on Taylor realising she is finally over an ex and no longer heartbroken. She uses water imagery, as the song opens with a drought, presumably symbolising the end of the relationship, before there is a gathering storm and then a downpour, which leaves her completely clean. The song was intended to be about love, but some lyrics can be interpreted as a reference to addiction and sobriety: "Ten months sober, I must admit, just because you're clean don't mean you don't miss it."

— ✦ —

RIGHT Welcome to New York! Taylor poses overlooking the city from the Empire State Building's private balcony in August 2014.

Dimitrios Kambouris/LP5/TAS Rights Management/Getty Images.

"I've told you my stories for years now. Some have been about coming of age. Some have been about coming undone. This is a story about coming into your own, and as a result... coming alive."

—✦—

LEFT Despite playing in huge stadiums, Taylor planned the show and staging to ensure the 1989 World Tour still felt like an intimate experience.

REPUTATION

Making a departure from her usual sunny disposition, Taylor returned from her time out of the spotlight with a darker sound

RELEASE DATE 10 NOVEMBER 2017

...READY FOR IT?

In the opening track, Taylor takes on the persona of a robber who is "stealing hearts and running off and never sayin' sorry." She meets her perfect partner in crime who will "join the heist" and escape to an island with her. This album was written in the early days of Taylor's relationship with Joe Alwyn, so many of the love songs on *reputation* are thought to refer to him. In the lyrics, Taylor states how their love is different to her other romances: "Every love I've known in comparison is a failure." The song features sexually suggestive lyrics, Taylor rapping in the verses, and references to the classic Hollywood couple Richard Burton and Elizabeth Taylor.

END GAME (FEAT. ED SHEERAN AND FUTURE)

Taylor reunited with Ed Sheeran, her duet partner on 2012 track 'Everything Has Changed', once again for 'End Game', which also features a verse from rapper Future. The song focuses on Taylor wanting a lover to be the person she ends up with for the rest of her life, with her singing that she doesn't want to be "just another ex-love you don't wanna see." In the track, Taylor acknowledges her "reputation precedes" her and assumes her lover has already been told she's "crazy".

I DID SOMETHING BAD

Just like 'Blank Space', Taylor leans into the character she was given by the media and public and sings from that perspective, with the chorus containing the lyrics: "They say I did something bad, but why's it feel so good? Most fun I ever had, and I'd do it over and over and over again if I could." This song features heavy electronic and trap elements, as well as an expletive – a rare occurrence in her music at the time. The post-chorus effect was created using Taylor's pitched-down voice as producer Martin couldn't find an instrument to achieve the sound she wanted. This song is thought to make reference to Kanye West and her ex-boyfriend Calvin Harris.

DON'T BLAME ME

In this midtempo track, Taylor compares being in love to a drug addiction, with her singing that love has made her crazy, and "My drug is my baby, I'll be usin' for the rest of my life." She continues the metaphor in the bridge when she sings "I get so high" and describes their romance as the "trip of my life". She also continues to play into the media's perception of her love life as she sings about "Toyin' with them older guys, just playthings for me to use." Many fans and critics have noted this track's sonic similarities to Hozier's 'Take Me to Church'.

DELICATE

Taylor sounds remarkably different on the sixth single, as she used a vocoder to give her voice a vulnerable and emotional quality, marking the first time she appears unguarded on the album. In all the tracks before 'Delicate', Taylor is strong and feisty, telling listeners she doesn't care about what people say about her. In contrast, here she is hesitant and questions how her reputation will affect the beginning of a new relationship. She wonders how much her lover has already heard about her, and whether it will cloud his judgement. Key lyrics include: "My reputation's never been worse, so you must like me for me."

LOOK WHAT YOU MADE ME DO

The album's lead single was a huge departure from any of Taylor's previous music and firmly established her new darker sound. She used the track to declare she was a new person, thanks to the lyrics: "The old Taylor can't come to the phone right now. Why? Oh, 'cause she's dead!" The song appears to reference her feud with Kanye West and the damage done to her reputation as a result of it, with lyrics such as, "I don't trust nobody and nobody trusts me." Members of British band Right Said Fred are credited as songwriters because her repetitive, almost-spoken chorus incorporates the melody of their 1991 song 'I'm Too Sexy'.

SO IT GOES...

This is one of the more sexually suggestive songs in Taylor's back catalogue, with lyrics including: "I'm not a bad girl, but I'll do bad things with you" and "Scratches down your back now…" It is thought to be about Alwyn, with the lyrics describing how they only have eyes for each other and get "caught up in a moment" when they're together, but "break down a little" when they're apart.

GORGEOUS

Taylor returns to her more conventional upbeat pop sound in this track, which opens with James, daughter of Ryan Reynolds and Blake Lively, saying the word 'gorgeous'. The song is about getting a crush even though she is in a relationship with somebody else, with the lyrics explaining: "And I got a boyfriend, he's older than us, he's in the club doing, I don't know what." Despite her relationship status, she's annoyed she's not with the object of her affection, as she sings: "You've ruined my life, by not being mine."

GETAWAY CAR

In this track, Taylor uses the imagery of criminals escaping a crime scene in a getaway car as a metaphor for a romance that was doomed from the start. The lyrics can be interpreted as a reference to her short-lived rebound romance with actor Tom Hiddleston, with her likening him to a getaway car speeding her away from her relationship with Calvin Harris. She knew the romance didn't have a real shot because of how it began, with her singing: "Should've known I'd be the first to leave, think about the place where you first met me."

LEFT Despite the album's 'darker' tone and aesthetic, thematically many of the songs are about love.

"Taylor was influenced by *Game of Thrones* when she wrote *reputation*"

KING OF MY HEART

The song has a unique structure where each section depicts the progression of a relationship. The first verse describes Taylor being happy on her own before her new lover comes along, then the pre-chorus represents them falling in love. The chorus shows their love getting deeper and more serious, with the lyrics: "And all at once, you're all I want, I'll never let you go, king of my heart, body, and soul." The accompanying music also radically changes throughout each stage. Taylor was influenced by *Game of Thrones* when she wrote *reputation* and wanted the post-chorus drum beat to sound like Dothraki drums.

DANCING WITH OUR HANDS TIED

This song depicts the early stages of Taylor's relationship with Alwyn, when she loved him "in secret" and the public didn't know about it yet. Much like 'I Know Places' on *1989*, this track details her fears about fame and the scrutiny surrounding her life ruining the romance once it gets discovered. Key lyrics include: "People started talking, putting us through our paces, I knew there was no one in the world who could take it, I had a bad feeling." The lyrics used in the title suggest they are having fun but lack the freedom and control that a normal couple would have.

DRESS

'Dress' is perhaps the most overtly sexual song Taylor has written at this point, with her revealing that she only brought the dress mentioned in the title so her man would take it off. The line, "I don't want you like a best friend," sparked a lot of debate regarding the subject of the song, with Sheeran being the prime suspect, but the track is once again about Alwyn. It seems to depict the stage in their relationship when they transitioned from friends to lovers, but nobody else knew, and she seemingly struggled to keep her attraction to him a secret.

THIS IS WHY WE CAN'T HAVE NICE THINGS

This light-hearted track opens with Taylor referring to the star-studded parties she used to throw for her 'squad' before the media turned on her for them. It also features one of the most specific references to her feud with West and his wife Kim Kardashian – "Friends don't try to trick you, get you on the phone and mind-twist you" – and touches upon her ruined reputation, with her praising her "real friends" and boyfriend for paying no attention to the gossip. She adds a comic touch by laughing after singing the words, "'Cause forgiveness is a nice thing to do" and saying, "I can't even say it with a straight face."

CALL IT WHAT YOU WANT

This slow spare ballad is set in the months Taylor stepped out of the public eye in 2016. Although her reputation was in tatters, she was doing just fine because she was falling in love with Alwyn, and the criticism "fades to nothing" when she's with him. The most poignant lyrics include: "My castle crumbled overnight" and "all the liars are calling me one," which refers to her public fall from grace. However, despite this, she insists, "I'm doing better than I ever was" due to her new romance.

NEW YEAR'S DAY

In contrast to the electro-pop that dominates the record, this song is a simple piano-led ballad. It is set the day after a big New Year's Eve party and features Taylor singing about being there to kiss Alwyn at midnight and also to clear up the mess the following day, meaning they will be both there during each other's highs and lows. Taylor can tell it's going "to be a long road" with him and hopes it doesn't ever come to an end, with the most telling lyrics including: "Please don't ever become a stranger whose laugh I could recognise anywhere."

LEFT Taylor on stage during the Reputation Stadium Tour show in Chicago, June 2018.

"We think we know
someone, but the truth
is that we only know the
version of them they have
chosen to show us."

—✦—

LEFT Taylor explained that *reputation* was her first album that people
didn't really 'get' until they saw her perform it live. The award-winning
Reputation Stadium Tour broke many box office records.

Quote from Taylor's *reputation* album liner notes, 2017
Image: Matt Winkelmeyer/TAS18/TAS Rights Management/Getty Images

LOVER

Taylor's seventh album was a celebration of love and marked
a return to a happier and more upbeat electro-pop sound

RELEASE DATE 23 AUGUST 2019

I FORGOT THAT YOU EXISTED

In the opening track, Taylor makes it clear that she has drawn a line under the events that inspired the dark tone of *reputation*. She recalls how much time she spent thinking about the person who had wronged her, presumably referring to Kanye West, and how she "lived in the shade you were throwing, 'til all of my sunshine was gone." She has found that her life is much better now she's let it go and considers that person with indifference. The carefree, upbeat song has a minimalist arrangement, with the vocals being accompanied by short piano chords and finger clicks.

CRUEL SUMMER

In this breezy pop track, Taylor sings about falling in love with a "bad boy" she is having a casual summer fling with. She's uncertain about the relationship's future and is desperately pining for something more. In the iconic bridge, she finally confesses her feelings: "And I scream for whatever it's worth, 'I love you, ain't that the worst thing you ever heard?'" The music was written by Jack Antonoff in collaboration with Annie Clark (aka St. Vincent). 'Cruel Summer' was originally set to be a single to promote *Lover*, but the Covid pandemic led to a change of plans. As a fan favourite, it had a resurgence in popularity thanks to The Eras Tour, and was finally released as a single in 2023.

LOVER

The album's title track and third single is a slow, romantic waltz with a nostalgic, timeless feel. Taylor wrote the acoustic guitar-led ballad, which describes her love for Alwyn, on her own the night before a studio session with Antonoff and they wanted to accompany the confessional lyrics with music that could have been played at a 1970s wedding reception. The lyrics in the bridge sound similar to wedding vows, with the lines: "Ladies and gentlemen, will you please stand? […] I take this magnetic force of a man to be my lover."

THE MAN

In the album's fourth single, Taylor addresses the sexism and double standards she has experienced during her career. She imagines how differently she would have been perceived and treated by the press and the public if she had been a man – and made the same choices in her life – with key lyrics including: "I'd be fearless leader, I'd be an alpha type. When everyone believes ya, what's that like?"

RIGHT Emerging from the darker aesthetic of *reputation*, Taylor's *Lover* era was dominated by pretty pastels and vibrant colours.

THE ARCHER

This deeply personal and honest song continues Taylor's tradition of making the fifth track her most vulnerable. It is a spare and minimalist midtempo song featuring heavy synths and soft house beats which build to create a sense of urgency. In the poetic lyrics, Taylor reflects on her flaws in past relationships and her insecurities about her new one.

I THINK HE KNOWS

This track's simple backing track evolves into a catchy, funk-inspired groove at the chorus. Taylor sings about how she and her lover are mutually obsessed with each other, and she doesn't need to admit how much she's into him because he already knows. The reference to "16th Avenue" refers to Music Row in Nashville, where Taylor used to write songs earlier in her career.

MISS AMERICANA & THE HEARTBREAK PRINCE

'Miss Americana…', which inspired the name of Taylor's 2020 Netflix documentary, is set in a high school. Its slow, melancholic production is peppered with cheerleader chants and seems, on the surface, to tell the story of a high school romance, reminiscent of 'You Belong with Me'. However, Taylor wrote it shortly after the 2018 US midterm elections to express her disappointment in the state of US politics. This is best exemplified with the lyrics: "American glory, faded before me," and "I saw the scoreboard, and ran for my life." She makes it clear that she supports the Democrats with the line, "We're so sad, we paint the town blue" and ends on a hopeful note, as she's convinced that her team is going to win again one day.

PAPER RINGS

In this bubbly and upbeat pop song, Taylor considers how far she and Alwyn had come from the beginning of their relationship, when she initially gave him the cold shoulder. She reminisces about the fun memories they share, reaffirms her commitment to him, and confesses that even though she likes "shiny things", she'd be so willing to marry him that she would do it with homemade paper rings.

CORNELIA STREET

In the opening verse, Taylor sings, "'I rent a place on Cornelia Street,' I say casually in the car", referring to the apartment she briefly rented in Greenwich Village in 2016. The song, which Taylor wrote on her own, is about her never wanting a relationship to end and how she would never be able to walk down that street again if they broke up as it would bring back all the memories she has connected with the place. Towards the end of the song, windscreen wipers can be heard in the background, helping listeners conjure up the image of them in the car.

DEATH BY A THOUSAND CUTS

With this track, Taylor wanted to prove that she could still write a breakup song despite being in a loving relationship at the time. Instead of using a moment from her own life, she was inspired by the characters and dynamics in the 2019 Netflix film *Someone Great*, which follows a woman who is trying to cope with heartbreak after getting dumped by her long-term boyfriend. Taylor admitted the film affected her so much that she started having dreams about living through the same situation. She wrote the lyrics on her own before bringing them to a studio session with Antonoff.

Words by Hannah Wales. Image: Frazer Harrison/Getty Images.

LONDON BOY

This light-hearted song opens with a snippet of Idris Elba talking about driving around London on his scooter, which was taken from his appearance on *The Late Late Show with James Corden*. The track serves as a celebration of her beloved "London boy", in reference to Alwyn, and details some of their favourite things to do in the British capital, with her naming places such as Brixton, Highgate, Camden Market and Shoreditch, singing about watching rugby in a pub, using slang such as "mate" and "babes", and namechecking fashion designer Stella McCartney, who she worked with on a line of *Lover* merchandise. The track interpolates the rhythm from Cautious Clay's 'Cold War', so he is credited as a songwriter.

SOON YOU'LL GET BETTER (FEAT. THE CHICKS)

This extremely emotional and personal ballad features backing vocals from Taylor's country idols, The Chicks. It was written in response to Taylor's mother's second battle with cancer. In the song, she repeats to her mum that she'll get better "'Cause you have to", but it's as if she's trying to convince them both, wondering how she'll cope if her mother isn't around anymore.

FALSE GOD

This is a sensual R&B-influenced love song featuring a solo saxophone throughout. Taylor uses heavy religious imagery to describe the ups and downs in her relationship with Alwyn and how their love might be a false God, but they'd still worship it anyway. Notable lyrics include: "The altar is my hips" and "Make confessions and we're begging for forgiveness, got the wine for you."

YOU NEED TO CALM DOWN

Taylor takes a clear stand with the LGBTQ+ community in *Lover*'s second single, which is directed at internet trolls, cancel culture and homophobes. To those who waste energy writing hateful messages to strangers, she sings: "'Cause shade never made anybody less gay […] You need to just stop." She was inspired to write the song with Joel Little after realising that her support for the LGBTQ+ community hadn't been loud or obvious enough. The accompanying star-studded music video won the Video for Good award.

— ✦ —

RIGHT Taylor posing with her backing singers Jeslyn Gorman, Eliotte Nicole, Melanie Nyema and Kamilah Marshall at an event for *Lover*.

AFTERGLOW

In this track, Taylor recalls having a heated fight with her partner, apologises for hurting his feelings and asks for reassurance that he won't leave her, "even when I lose my mind". She takes responsibility for blowing something out of proportion, punishing him with silence and for being the one who "burned us down" and asks for forgiveness. Key lyrics include: "I don't want to do this to you" and "I don't want to lose this with you."

ME! (FEAT. BRENDON URIE)

This bubblegum pop song served as the lead single from *Lover* and reaffirmed Taylor's return to a more cheerful and upbeat tone. 'ME!' is all about embracing self-love, celebrating and owning your individuality. It is a duet between Taylor and Brendon Urie from Panic! at the Disco, who have both been fans of each other's work for years. They sing from both sides of a couple, each insisting the other will never do any better, with lyrics like: "I promise that you'll never find another like me."

IT'S NICE TO HAVE A FRIEND

This dreamy love ballad could be seen as a story of two childhood friends who embark on a romance and end up getting married, however, Taylor has clarified that it is about the feeling of finding a close friend at different times of your life, rather than one linear story. It begins with Taylor being nostalgic about childhood friendships and then comparing them to finding a friend in the person you love. This track is very different from Taylor's usual output in terms of instrumentation, as her vocals are accompanied by steel drums and harps (giving the song an almost music-box quality), as well as a trumpet solo and a choir of background vocals. It also samples 'Summer in the South', a track by The Regent Park School of Music youth choir in Toronto, Canada.

DAYLIGHT

Taylor considered calling the album *Daylight* for a while, but eventually went with *Lover*. She chose the ballad – which she wrote solo – as the album's closing track because it recognises the past damage and pain she's experienced in relationships, and the fact that she's finally decided to let it all go so she can experience the daylight with Alwyn. Forgiving herself for past mistakes, she sings: "I wounded the good and I trusted the wicked." It features a callback to her song 'Red' and concludes with a spoken word outro in which Taylor says she wants "to be defined by the things that I love."

"This album is a love letter to love itself – all the captivating, spellbinding, maddening, devastating red, blue, gray, golden aspects of it."

RIGHT Taylor at the 2019 iHeartRadio Wango Tango event in June 2019. Her planned Lover Fest tour unfortunately had to be cancelled due to the Covid pandemic.

FOLKLORE

Taylor's surprise lockdown album sees her effortlessly switch gear once again, leaving pop behind to produce a wistful, melancholic masterpiece

RELEASE DATE 24 JULY 2020

THE 1

The opening track sees Taylor contemplating a past relationship. While the verses are more upbeat – as she appreciates the good things she has and wishes her ex well – this positive outlook soon morphs into nostalgia and thoughts of 'what if' during the chorus: "If one thing had been different, would everything be different today?" Taylor's *folklore* collaborator, Aaron Dessner (of The National), revealed in an interview with *Vulture* that this track was actually a late addition: "'the 1' and 'hoax' were the last songs we did. The album was sort of finished before that […] These are the bookends, you know?"

CARDIGAN

This enchanting piano ballad is the first song in what Taylor calls the Teenage Love Triangle, a trio of interconnected tracks exploring a fictional high school romance from each person's point of view. Alongside 'august' and 'betty', 'cardigan' tells the story from Betty's perspective as she reflects on her relationship with James. Despite being heartbroken after he cheats on her, Betty knew he would return to her: "I knew you'd miss me once the thrill expired, and you'd be standing in my front porch light. And I knew you'd come back to me" – an event that's revisited from James' perspective later in the album.

THE LAST GREAT AMERICAN DYNASTY

This song describes the life of Rebekah Harkness, a wealthy heiress and patron of the arts whose eccentric behaviour earned her a scandalous reputation in high society. It is one of the more uptempo tracks on the album, with a jaunty syncopated beat driving the melody along. As the song progresses, the story becomes personal as Taylor draws parallels between Harkness and herself. Several years ago, Taylor bought the heiress' old Rhode Island mansion, Holiday House, and both women have received their unfair share of scrutiny from the media. Tongue in cheek, she triumphantly sings through the outro, "I had a marvellous time ruining everything."

EXILE (FEAT. BON IVER)

Taylor's raw and emotional duet with Bon Iver's Justin Vernon explores the moment a former couple see each other again for the first time after their breakup. We hear the pair's opposing perspectives on their relationship: Justin's character is bitter at how it seemingly ended out of the blue, while Taylor's character laments how many chances she gave their relationship before deciding to walk away. 'exile' is one of several tracks on *folklore* to use film-related metaphors to describe a relationship, a common motif in Taylor's songwriting.

MY TEARS RICOCHET

Sombre chords and ethereal backing vocals give 'my tears ricochet' a fitting funeral-like atmosphere. Taylor revealed that this was the first song she wrote for *folklore*, inspired by the idea of "an embittered tormentor showing up at the funeral of his fallen object of obsession." Some fans believe the metaphorical death Taylor sings about could actually be a reference to her decision to leave Big Machine Records, with the line "And when you can't sleep at night, you hear my stolen lullabies" alluding to Taylor's dispute with Scooter Braun and Scott Borchetta over the ownership of the masters for her first six albums.

BELOW Taylor surprised everyone when she announced *folklore* – even her record label didn't know until a few hours before release.

MIRRORBALL

Taylor compares herself to the titular 'mirrorball', seen as an object to entertain others and reflect the personalities of those around her. The line "I'm still trying everything to keep you looking at me" touches on a point Taylor made in *Miss Americana* about the unreasonable expectations for women in music to reinvent themselves to stay relevant: "The female artists that I know of, they've reinvented themselves twenty times more than the male artists. They have to, or else you're out of a job! Constantly having to reinvent, constantly finding new facets of yourself that people find to be shiny…"

SEVEN

Against a driving piano melody, the narrator reminisces about a childhood friendship with someone from a troubled home ("I think your house is haunted, your dad is always mad"). She recalls the methods of escapism children use in difficult situations, and the naïve ways they try to help ("I think you should come live with me and we can be pirates, then you won't have to cry or hide in the closet"). The line "Passed down like folk songs, our love lasts so long" is *folklore* in a nutshell; as Taylor explained in her album announcement notes, "A tale that becomes folklore is one that is passed down and whispered around."

AUGUST

The second part of the Teenage Love Triangle, told from the perspective of the girl James had a fling with (Taylor later revealed she calls her Augustine). She recalls their passionate affair and how it ended because James was still in love with Betty. Although James himself dismisses it as "just a summer thing" (in 'betty'), Augustine wishes their relationship could have developed into something more, with the hypnotic refrain: "For me it was enough to live for the hope of it all, cancelled plans just in case you'd call…"

THIS IS ME TRYING

On the surface, this song is about someone attempting to make amends after a relationship goes wrong, accepting responsibility for their mistakes. It touches on some dark themes surrounding the narrator's mental health, including depression and alcoholism: "They told me all of my cages were mental, so I got wasted like all my potential." But the 'relationship' could also symbolise Taylor's career – in particular her return from a self-imposed hiatus in 2016-17 ("I've been having a hard time adjusting […] Didn't know if you'd care if I came back") – and her struggles with living in the public eye.

Words by Tiffany Starlow. Image: TAS Rights Management 2021/Getty Images.

ILLICIT AFFAIRS

This isn't the first time Taylor has sung about infidelity, but 'illicit affairs' is a far more nuanced and almost sympathetic approach to the topic than the uncompromising standpoint of 'Should've Said No' from her debut album. It is sung from the perspective of someone trapped in an affair and the endless lies it entails, as she laments her situation but feels unable to escape it. Taylor's biting delivery during the bridge perfectly captures the character's conflicting emotions: "Don't call me 'kid', don't call me 'baby'. Look at this idiotic fool that you made me."

INVISIBLE STRING

The title of this song is a reference to the 'red thread of fate' from East Asian mythology – the belief that soul mates are bound by an invisible red cord, and destiny will bring them together. Over the sweet melody of finger-picked guitar, Taylor sings about how all the heartbreak of past relationships ultimately led her to finding happiness. Dessner explained in his interview with *Vulture* how he created the distinctive sound for what is arguably *folklore*'s most folk-like song: "It's played on this rubber bridge that my friend put on [the guitar] and it deadens the strings so that it sounds old."

MAD WOMAN

One of *folklore*'s darker tracks explores the idea that women are often unfairly dismissed as 'mad' whenever they are justifiably angry or upset. Taylor had previously spoken about this idea in a 2019 interview with *CBS Sunday Morning*: "A man is allowed to 'react'; a woman can only 'over-react'." Her delivery is haunting, and her lyrics scathing as she takes aim at 'witch hunters' and gaslighters. Speaking to *Vulture*, Dessner said: "It has a darkness that I think is cathartic […] It has this very sharp tone to it, but sort of in gothic folklore. It's this record's goth song."

EPIPHANY

'epiphany' is an ethereal ode to those on the front lines, past and present, and the idea that dreams can provide some temporary respite from the chaos. In the album announcement notes, Taylor mentions how the opening segments were inspired by her grandfather's experience serving in World War Two, while the second verse is a reference to the medics of the Covid-19 pandemic ("Hold your hand through plastic now"). Speaking to *Vulture*, Dessner explained how he gave the song its unique sound: "It's lots of different instruments played and then slowed down and reversed. […] It was very beautiful to get lost in."

BETTY

There are echoes of 'Love Story' in 'betty' – a catchy melody with country motifs, a charming narrative of the highs and lows of young romance, and a key change to make your heart soar. This is the final part of the Teenage Love Triangle trilogy, as we hear the course of events from James' perspective. He regrets his summer fling with Augustine and wonders whether Betty will ever forgive him for being unfaithful, as he never stopped loving her. The lyrics include several callbacks to both 'cardigan' and 'august' ("Standing in your cardigan, kissing in my car again" and "She pulled up like a figment of my worst intentions […] Slept next to her, but I dreamt of you all summer long") to weave the trilogy together.

PEACE

While several tracks on *folklore* are sung from the perspective of fictional characters, 'peace' appears to be one of the record's more personal songs. The lyrics allude to the impact Taylor's fame has on her love life, in particular her relationship with Joe Alwyn at the time. The stripped back production allows her thoughtful lyrics to shine through, as she confesses to her partner that – no matter how dedicated they are to one another – her career and celebrity status will inevitably cause complications and prevent them from having a 'normal' life together: "The devil's in the details but you got a friend in me. Would it be enough if I could never give you peace?"

HOAX

The album's closing track is a melancholic piano ballad reflecting on a troubled relationship. The lyrics describe someone committed to her partner even though their love seems hopeless and makes her miserable: "Don't want no other shade of blue but you. No other sadness in the world would do." Dessner gave his take on the song in his interview with *Vulture*, saying, "There's sadness, but it's a kind of hopeful sadness. It's a recognition that you take on the burden of your partners, your loved ones, and their ups and downs." This feeling of 'hopeful sadness' is one that *folklore* manages to capture, and is expressed so beautifully in many of its tracks. A perfect note for the album to end on.

—✦—

LEFT Along with *Lover*, *evermore* and *Midnights*, Taylor was finally able to bring *folklore* to life on stage during The Eras Tour. The seventh act embraces this album's ethereal, cottagecore aesthetic.

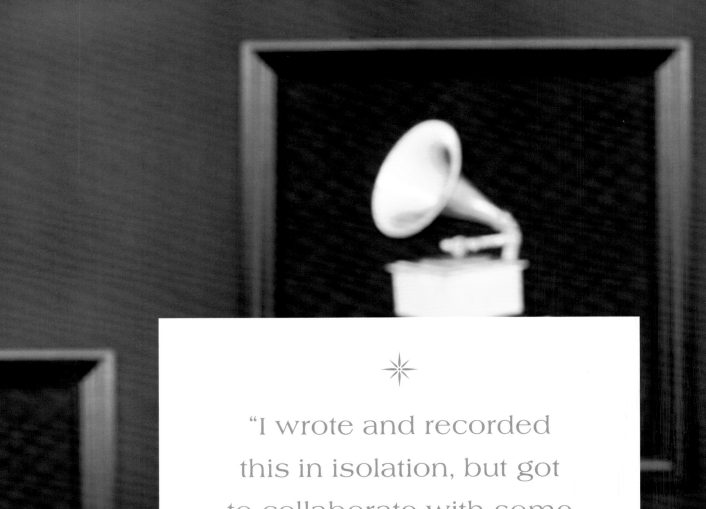

✦

"I wrote and recorded this in isolation, but got to collaborate with some musical heroes of mine."

—✦—

RIGHT Taylor won Album of the Year Grammy for *folklore*, making her the first woman in history to win that award three times.

ote from Taylor's *folklore* foreword. 2020.

age: Jay L. Clendenin/Los Angeles Times/Getty Images.

EVERMORE

Breaking from her tradition of treating albums like one-off eras, Taylor released *folklore*'s sister album just five months later, with more mesmerising stories

RELEASE DATE 11 DECEMBER 2020

WILLOW

Taylor picked 'willow' as the lead single from *evermore* because she liked the "witchy", "magical and mysterious" sound and thought it set the right tone for the album. It's about intrigue, desire and the complexity that goes into wanting someone, with Taylor's character seemingly unsure of her crush's feelings towards her. Taylor told fans on YouTube: "I think it sounds like casting a spell to make somebody fall in love with you."

CHAMPAGNE PROBLEMS

This song tells the story of a man getting down on one knee to propose to his college sweetheart in front of his family and friends, and the woman breaking his heart by saying no. Joe Alwyn, under his alias William Bowery, created the melodic structure of the song and Taylor wrote the lyrics. Taylor told Apple Music that this song has one of her favourite bridges because it "shifts gears" and tells the whole story; she couldn't wait to perform it in front of a crowd and hear everyone sing along.

RIGHT Taylor found that she "just couldn't stop writing songs" after *folklore*, so – in a career first – she decided to make a 'sister' album.

GOLD RUSH

In 'gold rush', the narrator is daydreaming about being in a relationship with a man who everybody wants to be with, but the dream fades as she realises "it could never be", since she wouldn't be able to handle the jealousy of being with such a heartthrob. Taylor wrote this chilled, dream-like song with Jack Antonoff, who also produced and provided background vocals, while his Bleachers bandmates played the instruments. It's one of *evermore*'s more pop-sounding tracks, with a pulsing beat and shifting tempo throughout, bookended with dreamy vocal segments.

'TIS THE DAMN SEASON

In the notes for *evermore*, Taylor revealed that this Christmassy track is a companion piece to 'dorothea' and depicts "what happens when she comes back for the holidays and rediscovers an old flame". Dorothea suggests to her hometown ex that they briefly rekindle their old romance before she goes back to Los Angeles, with key lyrics including "I'll be yours for the weekend" and "the road not taken looks real good now". Taylor wrote the song in the middle of the night after a day of rehearsing for the *folklore: the long pond studio sessions* film at Dessner's studio, and sang the lyrics to him in the kitchen the following morning.

"'champagne problems' has one of Taylor's favourite bridges... She couldn't wait to perform it in front of a crowd and hear everyone sing along"

—◆—

TOLERATE IT

Taylor continues her tradition of making track five her most vulnerable song with 'tolerate it', which is told from the perspective of a woman who loves her older partner but he just seems to be ambivalent towards her. Taylor was inspired by Daphne du Maurier's *Rebecca*, in which the lead character is essentially ignored by her husband after they return home from their honeymoon. Taylor told Apple Music, "There was a part of me that was relating to that because at some point in my life, I felt that way."

NO BODY, NO CRIME (FEAT. HAIM)

Taylor was inspired by her obsession with true crime stories and wrote a murder-mystery tale that revolves around a woman named Este, who confronts her cheating husband and suddenly goes missing, and the narrator is Este's friend who avenges her murder. Taylor wrote the song solo before reaching out to one of her best friends – Este Haim – to see if her band wanted to do backing vocals. Her namesake was already written in the lyrics, but the real Este got to pick the reference to the restaurant chain Olive Garden. The song features some country elements – a throwback to Taylor's roots – and marks her first collaboration with HAIM.

HAPPINESS

The deceptively titled 'happiness' tells the story of a woman who is adjusting to single life after "seven years in heaven" and trying to move on from the breakup and find "the new me". Despite the hurt and anger in the lyrics, it's ultimately a hopeful song. Dessner had been working on the instrumental since 2019, thinking it would be for Big Red Machine – his experimental folk-rock band with Bon Iver's Justin Vernon – but Taylor loved the music and wrote lyrics to it. It was the last song Taylor wrote for the album, and "the new me" line also reflects the reinvention she'll undergo after this chapter.

DOROTHEA

The companion piece to ''tis the damn season' is told from the male perspective, with Dorothea's ex wondering if she ever thinks about him back home in Tupelo after moving to LA to pursue her Hollywood dreams. The narrator is curious as to whether Dorothea is still the same person now she's got fortune and fame, and encourages her to "come back to my side". Taylor clarified in a YouTube comment that 'dorothea' doesn't continue *folklore's* Teenage Love Triangle, but in her mind "Dorothea went to the same school as Betty, James and Inez".

CONEY ISLAND (FEAT. THE NATIONAL)

This melancholic ballad tells the story of two exes who are sitting on a bench in Coney Island, a beachside fairground in New York, reminiscing about a past relationship and wondering where they went wrong. This marks Taylor's first collaboration with the whole of The National, not just Dessner. She originally wrote the lyrics with Alwyn and recorded it with just her voice, but they decided to get all of Dessner's bandmates involved, with lead singer Matt Berninger adding his vocals. Taylor told Apple Music she was thrilled to get her "favourite lead singer of (her) favourite band" to sing the words "happy birthday" on 'coney island', as *evermore* was released the week of her 31st birthday.

IVY

In this song, Taylor uses nature imagery to tell the story of a woman who is cheating on her husband and wondering what the husband will do if or when he finds out. Ivy is a fast-growing and notoriously hard-to-remove plant, so the metaphor implies that the narrator's secret affair is taking over, even though she knows it's a bad idea. In her message about *evermore* on social media, Taylor revealed 'ivy' was part of the "'unhappily ever after' anthology of marriages gone bad that includes infidelity, ambivalent toleration, and even murder", with the other two being 'tolerate it' and 'no body, no crime'. The song was written by Taylor, Dessner and Antonoff, and has subtle backing vocals from Vernon.

COWBOY LIKE ME

This track is about two young con artists who meet while "hanging out at fancy resorts trying to score rich romantic beneficiaries", according to Taylor's album notes. They fall in love and put their old scamming lifestyles behind them. The song features background vocals from Marcus Mumford of Mumford & Sons, who Taylor is a big fan of, and a guitar solo by Vernon.

LONG STORY SHORT

The only uptempo pop song on *evermore* revisits themes from the *reputation* era and refers to when Taylor left the public eye in 2016 following her feud with Kanye West and his then wife Kim Kardashian, with notable lyrics including: "And I fell from the pedestal, right down the rabbit hole, long story short, it was a bad time." Taylor "survived" that chapter and has moved on from "keeping score" and is now "all about you", presumably referring to Alwyn. She also offers up advice to her past self and tells her "not to get lost in these petty things".

MARJORIE

This track is about Taylor's grandmother Marjorie Finlay, an opera singer who passed away in 2003 when Taylor was 13. The song features Taylor thinking about advice she learned from her grandmother and how she regrets not fully appreciating who Finlay was because she was too young. Taylor admitted to Apple Music that she was a "wreck at times" when she wrote the song and found it hard to sing it without a catch in her throat because she was so emotional. She sent Dessner some of Finlay's opera recordings and he sampled them in the song, so Finlay is credited with background vocals. 'marjorie' is track 13 on *evermore*, while 'epiphany', which was inspired by Taylor's late grandfather, is track 13 on *folklore*.

CLOSURE

This experimental song, which has an unusual time signature, depicts the narrator receiving a letter from an estranged friend or ex who is reaching out to achieve closure and suggest they remain friends, but she isn't interested in ironing out their differences and is "fine with my spite". Vernon put Taylor's vocals through his vocal modifier to distort her sound. Dessner revealed in an interview with *Billboard* that Taylor originally wrote 'closure' and 'dorothea' for Big Red Machine, his band with Vernon. He explained: "The more I listened to them, not that they couldn't be Big Red Machine songs, but they felt like interesting, exciting Taylor songs."

EVERMORE (FEAT. BON IVER)

The album's title track, a piano ballad, is Taylor's second duet with Justin Vernon after their *folklore* collaboration 'exile'. In the beginning, the narrator has "been down" for months and feels like their pain, or perhaps depression, will be "for evermore". However, it ends with the narrator feeling a glimmer of hope. Much like 'exile', Alwyn composed the piano part and Taylor wrote the lyrics, while Vernon subsequently added the bridge. This time, Alwyn was also able to play the piano for the recording remotely. Similar to 'hoax' closing its sister album, this song brings *evermore* to an end with a similar note of 'hopeful sadness', providing listeners with a thoughtful finale to another wonderfully wistful record.

— ✦ —

RIGHT Taylor and HAIM on stage during Eras. Taylor has joked that she's the "fourth Haim sister". As well as 'no body, no crime', in 2021 she collaborated on a remix of their song 'Gasoline'.

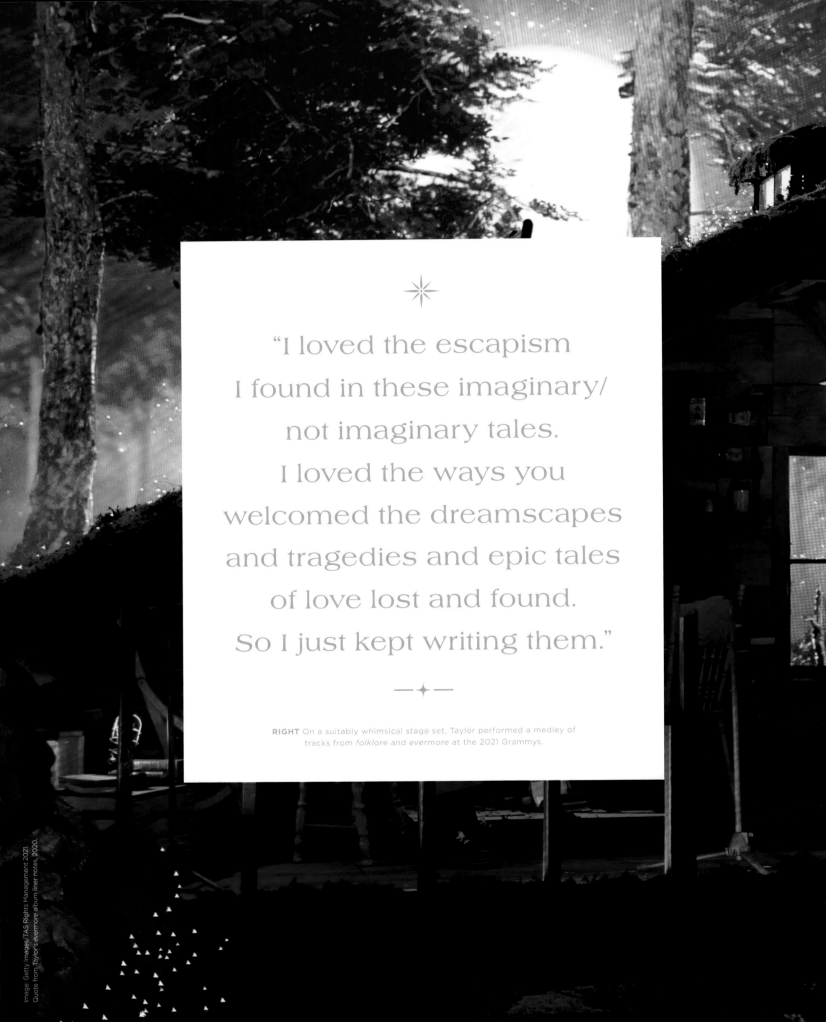

✦

"I loved the escapism
I found in these imaginary/
not imaginary tales.
I loved the ways you
welcomed the dreamscapes
and tragedies and epic tales
of love lost and found.
So I just kept writing them."

— ✦ —

RIGHT On a suitably whimsical stage set, Taylor performed a medley of
tracks from *folklore* and *evermore* at the 2021 Grammys.

MIDNIGHTS

Returning to pop after a two-record folk detour, Taylor made a concept album inspired "by the stories of 13 sleepless nights"

RELEASE DATE 21 OCTOBER 2022

LAVENDER HAZE

Taylor first heard the common 1950s phrase "lavender haze" while watching *Mad Men* and discovered it meant being in an "all-encompassing love glow". She sings about doing everything she can to keep her relationship in that blissful state, such as ignoring outside opinions and tabloid gossip. Taylor seemingly also addresses the frequent speculation that she was engaged to her then boyfriend Joe Alwyn by singing, "All they keep asking me is if I'm gonna be your bride". The lyrics are reminiscent of 'Delicate' as Taylor praises her partner for how well he handled all the media attention surrounding her life at the time. Taylor's good friend, actress Zoë Kravitz, served as a co-writer on the song, and also provided backing vocals.

MAROON

A call-back to the title of her 2012 album and song 'Red', 'Maroon' sees Taylor reminiscing about the highs and lows she experienced throughout a failed relationship, admitting that she still thinks about it. During the bridge, she cathartically sings: "And I wake with your memory over me, that's a real f***ing legacy to leave." Maroon and burgundy are darker than the "burning red" in 'Red', which suggest a more mature love than the kind she examined a decade before.

ANTI-HERO

In the album's chart-topping lead single, Taylor gets candid about her insecurities. She explained on social media that this is one of her favourite songs because it's "really honest" about her self-criticism: "I really don't think I've delved this far into my insecurities in this much detail before." She described the track as a "guided tour" of the things she hates about herself, admitting that she struggles with not feeling like a real person and how her life has become "unmanageably sized". You can draw some parallels between 'Anti-Hero' and 'The Archer', from *Lover*, because they both feature confessional lyrics about self-loathing.

SNOW ON THE BEACH (FEAT. LANA DEL REY)

This dreamy pop ballad features backing vocals from Lana Del Rey. Taylor told her fans that she will be "grateful for life" that Lana agreed to appear on the song, as she considers her "one of the best musical artists ever". The song is about the surreal moment where two people fall in love with each other at the exact same time. Lana explained that she matched Taylor's vocals in the original version to blend their voices seamlessly together. Despite this, fans wanted to hear more from her, so the duo released another version where Lana takes the lead on the second verse.

> "Taylor explained on social media that 'Anti-Hero' is one of her favourite songs because it's 'really honest' about her self-criticism"

YOU'RE ON YOUR OWN, KID

Taylor's fifth track starts with a recollection of an early hometown relationship, before morphing into a tale about the beginnings of her career and the struggles she faced in her rise to fame. The song can be interpreted as a message from Taylor to her younger self. She candidly references her past eating disorder in the bridge. She also admits to burning some bridges to get ahead with the lyrics: "'Cause there were pages turned with the bridges burned, everything you lose is a step you take." The track begins with a pulsing beat that builds throughout.

MIDNIGHT RAIN

Accompanied by a minimalist drum beat and synth sounds, Taylor reflects on a past relationship that ended because she wanted to pursue her career instead of settling down. She recalls how they were the opposites of each other – with him being the "sunshine" and her the "midnight rain" – and how they had different expectations of the relationship. He wanted to get married, whereas she was more focused on her work; she wanted to grow and evolve while he was happy with the status quo.

QUESTION...?

In the seventh track, Taylor asks her ex a series of questions about their time together, wondering if every relationship he has been in since then has felt inferior. She asks if he regrets not putting up more of a fight at the end of their romance and if he wishes he could still touch her. The song begins with an interpolation of Taylor's 2016 single 'Out of the Woods', which is also about a failed relationship. Actor Dylan O'Brien, Jack Antonoff, his sister Rachel and Taylor's brother Austin provided crowd noises for the song.

VIGILANTE SHIT

This trap-oriented track tells the story of a woman on a quest for revenge after a man does her wrong. She also helps other scorned women "get even" with liars and cheats, singing, "She needed cold, hard proof, so I gave her some (…) Now she gets the house, gets the kids, gets the pride." The song could have easily fit in with the dark revenge theme of *reputation*, while it also parallels the story of vigilante justice that Taylor tells in 'no body, no crime' from *evermore*.

LEFT Taylor closes her Eras shows with the *Midnights* act, where the big finale is a celebratory dance party to 'Karma'.

Words by Hannah Wales. Image: Scott Eisen/TAS23/TAS Rights Management/Getty Images.

"Fans once speculated that Taylor had made an album called *Karma* after the word appeared in the music video for 'The Man' in early 2020, but – at least so far – this has not materialised"

BEJEWELED

In this bubblegum pop song, Taylor expresses her frustrations with a lover who has been taking her for granted and not treating her the way she deserves. Knowing her self-worth, she goes on a night out to regain her confidence and prove she's still got what it takes to "make the whole place shimmer". She admitted to iHeartRadio that the song is also her way of "hyping myself up to return to pop music" and checking to see if she is still dazzling enough for pop after her folk albums.

LABYRINTH

Taylor sings about entering into a new relationship with some hesitancy in this track's hazy dreamscape. With her breathy, ethereal vocals, she reveals how she was still hurting from a past breakup when she met her new lover. The pain was so great that Taylor assumed she would never be able to move on, but then all of a sudden she finds herself falling for someone new. With the contrariety in the line "Oh no, I'm falling in love again", it seems her open heart and the maze of her mind are in conflict – she's happy to be in love, but there is trepidation; she wants to protect herself from falling too quickly.

KARMA

Taylor reflects on how karma has served her well, as she is happy with her life and wonders if her detractors can say the same. She told iHeartRadio that this song "is written from a perspective of feeling really happy, really proud of the way your life is, feeling like this must be a reward for doing stuff right." Taylor has explored the concept of karma throughout her discography. Fans once speculated that she had made an album called *Karma* after the words appeared in the music video for 'The Man' in early 2020, but – at least so far – this has not materialised.

SWEET NOTHING

Taylor wrote this dreamy pop ballad with Alwyn under his William Bowery pseudonym, which he previously used for their collaborations on *folklore* and *evermore*. The track reflects on how simple, easy and calm their relationship was at home, in contrast to their hectic public lives. She finds peace knowing that her partner wants "sweet nothing" from her while she faces pressure and high expectations from the outside world. The title has a double meaning, as 'sweet nothings' also describes words of affection exchanged between lovers. In the opening verse, Taylor references collecting a pebble from a shore in County Wicklow in Ireland, where Alwyn filmed the 2022 TV drama, *Conversations with Friends*.

MASTERMIND

In the standard edition's closing track, Taylor confesses that it was not fate or luck that brought her and a lover together – it was actually the result of her calculated scheming. The lyrics contrast the theme of destiny in love, illustrated in previous songs such as 'invisible string'. In the standout confessional moment in the track, Taylor sings, "No one wanted to play with me as a little kid, so I've been scheming like a criminal ever since." She told iHeartRadio that the song is like the "romantic version" of the strategies she usually uses when planting Easter eggs for her fans. She explained, "You have been planning and plotting things and making them look like an accident — and I think that's sort of an inside joke between me and my fans, that I tend to do that."

LEFT Taylor announced *Midnights* at the MTV Video Music Awards while accepting the award for Video of the Year in August 2022.

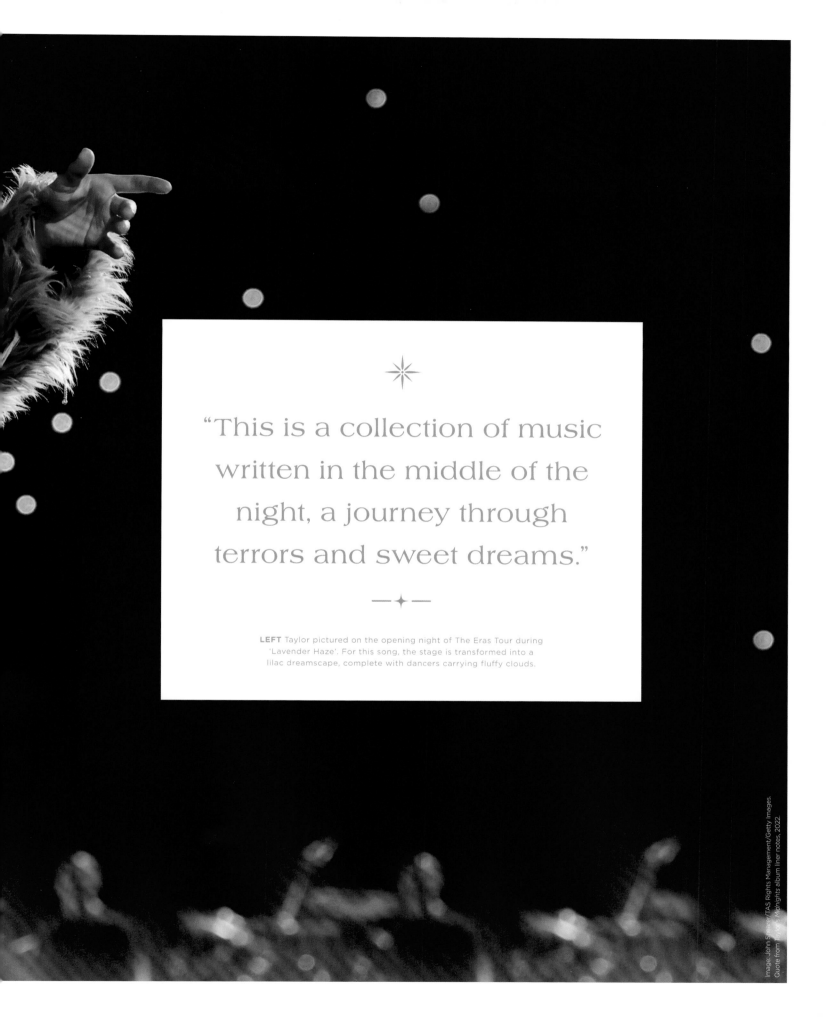

"This is a collection of music written in the middle of the night, a journey through terrors and sweet dreams."

—✦—

LEFT Taylor pictured on the opening night of The Eras Tour during 'Lavender Haze'. For this song, the stage is transformed into a lilac dreamscape, complete with dancers carrying fluffy clouds.

Isaac Brekken/AP Photo/Alamy.

43rd Annual Academy of Country Music Awards, Las Vegas NV, 18 May 2008.

Isaac Peter Kramer/AP Photo/Alamy.

Larry Busacc/Erickson Public/Getty Images.

MTV Video Music Awards, New York City NY, 13 September 2009.

Backstage on the Fearless Tour, New York City NY, 27 August 2009.

Country Music Association Fan Fest, Nashville TN, 12 June 2011.

Photoshoot session, Hollywood CA, 22 September 2010.

Taylor and Shania Twain, filming in Thompson's Station TN, 6 June 2011.

MTV Video Music Awards, Los Angeles CA, 6 September 2012.

The Victoria's Secret Fashion Show, New York City NY, 13 November 2013.

Z100 Jingle Ball, New York City NY, 12 December 2014.

Vanity Fair Oscar Party, Beverly Hills CA, 28 February 2016.

The Reputation Stadium Tour, Arlington TX, 6 October 2018.

Camila Cabello, Taylor and Halsey performing at the American Music Awards, Los Angeles CA, 24 November 2019.

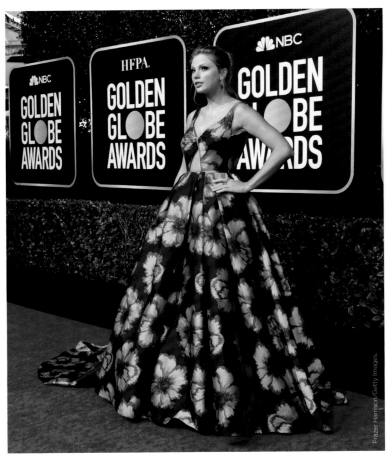

77th Annual Golden Globe Awards, Beverly Hills CA, 5 January 2020.

The Grammy Awards, Los Angeles CA, 14 March 2021.

New York University commencement ceremony, New York City NY, 18 May 2022.

Opening night of The Eras Tour, Glendale AZ, 17 March 2023.

Beyoncé's *Renaissance* film premiere, London, 30 November 2023.

Taylor with some of her dancers during The Eras Tour, Sydney, 23 February 2024.

taylor's version

FEARLESS

Taylor kickstarted her album re-recording project by revisiting
her second studio album, 13 years after its original release

RELEASE DATE 9 APRIL 2021

A couple of months after Scott Borchetta sold the master recordings of Taylor's first six albums – her 2006 self-titled debut through to 2017's *reputation* – to Scooter Braun, Taylor announced that she would re-record them so she could regain ownership and control of her music.

Rather than start at the beginning and re-record *Taylor Swift* first, she announced in February 2021 that she would kick off her re-recording project with *Fearless*, which scored Taylor her first Album of the Year Grammy back in 2008.

Not content with simply redoing the 13 tracks on the original album, Taylor re-recorded the 19 songs on the platinum edition of *Fearless*, 'Today Was a Fairytale' from the *Valentine's Day* movie soundtrack, and six 'From the Vault' tracks that "killed [her] to leave behind" when she made the album in 2008.

Taylor recruited her usual collaborators Jack Antonoff and Aaron Dessner as well as touring musicians from the *Fearless* era for the project, and she was determined to stay true to the lyrics, melodies and arrangements of the originals but improve upon their sonic quality.

"We really did go in and try to create a 'the same but better' version," she explained on *PEOPLE*. "I did go in line by line and listen to every single vocal… If I can improve upon it, I did. But I really did want this to be very true to

what I initially thought of and what I had initially written. But better. Obviously."

This has resulted in a replica of *Fearless* that may seem identical to the uninitiated, but has subtle differences that fans who grew up with the original will notice and appreciate. For example, Taylor's vocals are stronger and more mature, the production is more polished and the quality of the recording itself has been improved.

Fans speculated that Taylor's next re-recording would be *Red* and, later that year, they were proved right…

YOU ALL OVER ME
(FEAT. MAREN MORRIS)

'You All Over Me' is about Taylor not being able to get over an ex following the end of a relationship, with her using similar imagery to 'Clean' from *1989*. Key lyrics include: "No amount of freedom gets you clean, I've still got you all over me." She called upon country singer Maren Morris – who made a surprise appearance on the Reputation Stadium Tour – to sing background vocals on the track. Taylor told her Instagram followers that she enjoyed being able to experiment and "include some of my favorite artists" on the final six tracks as they had never been heard before.

MR. PERFECTLY FINE

Another breakup song, 'Mr. Perfectly Fine' is widely believed to be about Joe Jonas, who Taylor dated briefly in 2008. In the track, Taylor speaks directly to a recent ex who dumped her without explanation. She seems to resent him for being "perfectly fine" after their split and moving on quickly with a new girl while she's still heartbroken. Taylor notably calls the ex "casually cruel", a description also used in 'All Too Well' from *Red*. Jonas' then wife, Sophie Turner, showed her support for the track on Instagram Stories, writing: "It's not NOT a bop."

WE WERE HAPPY

In this ballad, Taylor speaks to an ex and reminisces about the halcyon days of their relationship. She recruited country singer Keith Urban, whose tour she opened back in 2009, to sing the harmony on this track. Taylor wrote on Instagram about their collaborations: "I'm really honored that @keithurban is a part of this project, duetting on 'That's When' and singing harmonies on 'We Were Happy'. I was his opening act during the *Fearless* album era and his music has inspired me endlessly."

THAT'S WHEN (FEAT. KEITH URBAN)

Her next collaboration with Urban is a duet that tells the story of a girl who leaves her boyfriend as she needs time and space "to think about all of this" and her asking when she can come back. Speaking about their collaboration on *The Ellen DeGeneres Show*, Urban revealed Taylor reached out to him about working together while he was Christmas shopping in Australia. He recalled: "I'm sitting in the food court at the shopping centre, listening to these two unreleased Taylor Swift songs. It was an unusual place to be hearing unreleased Taylor Swift music but I loved the songs and luckily got to put a vocal on both of those."

DON'T YOU

'Don't You' has a similar theme to 'Mr. Perfectly Fine' in that Taylor is still in love with an ex and he's already moved on with someone else. The exes are seeing each other in public for the first time since the split, and Taylor hates that he's being so nice and friendly to her when he caused her so much heartache – even though she doesn't hate him, she doesn't want to pretend to be friends. Taylor told Spotify that this was a "really fun song" to write with Tommy Lee James because there was "a wellspring of emotion to draw from". She also praised producer Jack Antonoff for "letting it just be really airy and sort of like a dreamscape".

BYE BYE BABY

The narrator of this track is driving away from her former boyfriend's home after just breaking up with him. She felt so sure that they'd always have a perfect relationship, but with a heavy heart she accepted that it wasn't working. A demo leaked years ago as 'The One Thing', but Taylor changed the title and some lyrics for its official release.

—✦—

LEFT On The Eras Tour, Taylor's outfits celebrate her past styles, like this flapper-inspired gold fringed dress for the *Fearless* section.

taylor's version

RED

Taylor revisits her 2012 album for the second instalment
in her ongoing album re-recording project

RELEASE DATE 12 NOVEMBER 2021

The second of Taylor's re-recorded albums, *Red (Taylor's Version)* features not only the 20 songs from the album's deluxe release, but also her 2012 charity single 'Ronan', her takes on 'Better Man' and 'Babe' (which she gave away to Little Big Town and Sugarland, respectively), and seven more 'From the Vault' tracks, including the 10-minute version of 'All Too Well'. Fans had been asking Taylor to release the fabled uncut version ever since she revealed that the song was originally far longer.

The majority of Taylor's original collaborators returned for the project, with the exception of producers Nathan Chapman and Max Martin. Much like *Fearless (Taylor's Version)*, Taylor's vocals here are stronger and more mature and the production is sharper, but otherwise, the re-recorded tracks are very loyal to the original versions, except for 'Girl at Home', which is now more of a pop song as the acoustic guitar instrumentation has been swapped for electronic sounds.

Taylor told talk show host Seth Meyers that she was thrilled to be able to dig up old songs from the archive and give them new life with collaborators such as Phoebe Bridgers and Chris Stapleton. Explaining why the tracks were originally cut, she said, "I wanted to save them for the next album and then it turned out the next album was a whole different thing and so they got left behind."

BETTER MAN

This track depicts Taylor missing a relationship and her ex, even though she knows she's "better off alone" since he was a jealous person who took her for granted. She sings, "We might still be in love, if you were a better man. You would've been the one, if you were a better man." After Taylor cut this song from the original *Red* album, she gave it to country group Little Big Town, who released it in 2016. It went on to win them a Grammy Award.

NOTHING NEW (FEAT. PHOEBE BRIDGERS)

This duet addresses anxieties over growing up, as the singers wonder if the public and music industry will still be interested in them when they're older, and a new, young and exciting artist comes on the scene. Taylor explained on *Late Night with Seth Meyers* that she wrote the song when she was 22 after she stopped feeling like "a shiny new artist". She wanted a female musician to duet with her and texted Phoebe Bridgers, who replied: "I've been waiting for this text my entire life."

RIGHT Taylor in her *Red*-style "A lot going on at the moment" T-shirt on the opening night of The Eras Tour.

BABE

In this country ballad, co-written with Patrick Monahan from Train, Taylor sings to a partner who has destroyed their relationship by being unfaithful. After it didn't make it onto the original cut of *Red*, she gave 'Babe' to country duo Sugarland, who released it in 2018, with her providing backing vocals and playing the 'other woman' in the music video. "I'm so happy that it gets its own life," Taylor said in an Instagram video when their version came out.

MESSAGE IN A BOTTLE

With this uptempo pop track, Taylor captures the anxiety and excitement of meeting a new crush and wondering if they'll become something more. It's the first track Taylor wrote with Max Martin and Shellback, her *1989* and *reputation* collaborators, and is rumoured to be about Harry Styles, due to the mention of London in the bridge.

I BET YOU THINK ABOUT ME (FEAT. CHRIS STAPLETON)

In this country-leaning song, Taylor sings about a relationship ending because her boyfriend felt their upbringings were "too different." She presumes that he still thinks of her despite being with someone else. Fans have speculated that the song is about Jake Gyllenhaal, as it mentions her ex growing up in Beverly Hills. Taylor wrote the track in June 2011 with Lori McKenna and they wanted to "make people laugh with it."

FOREVER WINTER

In this track, which Taylor co-wrote with Mark Foster from Foster the People, the narrator is constantly worrying and stressing about her partner's wellbeing as he seems to be struggling with his mental health. Key lyrics include, "I pull at every thread trying to solve the puzzles in his head," and "If I was standing there in your apartment, I'd take that bomb in your head and disarm it."

RUN (FEAT. ED SHEERAN)

In her second duet with Ed Sheeran on the album, they sing about getting out of town and going where "no one else is." It was the first song they ever wrote together and 'Everything Has Changed' – an original *Red* track – followed around a week later. Ed told Capital FM that 'Run' was his favourite of the two and he always hoped it would resurface, saying: "I'm so happy it's seeing the light of day."

THE VERY FIRST NIGHT

In this dance-pop track, Taylor reminisces fondly about a past relationship and wishes she could go "back in time" to the night they met as she misses him so much. Taylor wrote this song with Espen Lind and Amund Bjørklund of Norwegian songwriting and production duo Espionage.

ALL TOO WELL (10 MINUTE VERSION)

The crown jewel of the *Red* re-release is the extended version of this fan-favourite ballad, which features more verses and a long outro. The song is widely accepted to be about Gyllenhaal. Taylor told talk show host Jimmy Fallon that she was excited for her fans to hear all the original lyrics. She said she turned up "really sad and upset" to rehearsals one day and "started ad-libbing what I was going through, and what I was feeling, and it went on, and the song kept building and building and building in intensity, and the song just went on for about 10 to 15 minutes of us doing this." Taylor believes that this will become the definitive version of the song.

taylor's version

SPEAK NOW

By revisiting her third studio album, Taylor was officially halfway
through her mission to remake her first six records

RELEASE DATE 7 JULY 2023

A country-pop album that also embraces a pop-rock sound, *Speak Now* was written solely by Taylor – a response to the critics who had claimed that she did not write her own songs. Announcing this Taylor's Version on social media (after first revealing it on tour), Taylor explained that "the songs that came from this time in my life were marked by their brutal honesty, unfiltered diaristic confessions and wild wistfulness. I love this album because it tells a tale of growing up, flailing, flying and crashing… and living to speak about it."

Alongside the 14 songs from the standard edition of *Speak Now* and two tracks ('Ours' and 'Superman') from the deluxe edition, Taylor also added six extra 'From the Vault' tracks. She reunited with longtime collaborators Jack Antonoff and Aaron Dessner to produce these new bonus songs.

Taylor's vocals are more mature and polished, which is hardly a surprise considering the original *Speak Now* was released in 2010. While most songs vary ever so slightly in length compared to the originals, the most notable difference in this re-recording is the lyric change in 'Better than Revenge'. Taylor has changed the original controversial line "She's better known for the things that she does on the mattress" to "He was a moth to the flame, she was holding the matches."

ELECTRIC TOUCH (FEAT. FALL OUT BOY)

The first of two collaborations on the album, this pop-punk track with a cinematic production sees Taylor and Patrick Stump, lead singer of Fall Out Boy, explore the uncertainty and giddiness ahead of a first date, as well as the hope of new love after experiencing heartbreak, "All I know is this could either break my heart or bring it back to life." This song was not the first time that she had joined forces with Fall Out Boy, as they previously performed together during the 2013 Victoria's Secret Fashion Show, and Stump made a special guest appearance during Taylor's Red Tour.

WHEN EMMA FALLS IN LOVE

This sweet and poignant song was co-produced with Dessner and follows the journey of Emma, a captivating young woman who falls in and out of love, ultimately finding her true love in the end. Swaying between a ballad with a piano melody to a country-pop song backed by guitars, the song expresses Taylor's admiration for her friend and is complemented by her heartfelt vocals. After the album's release, Taylor revealed during her first show in Kansas City for the Eras Tour that this song was written about one of her best friends, further fuelling existing speculation that the 'Emma' in question is her close friend, actress Emma Stone.

I CAN SEE YOU

A sultry and sexy tune that is filled with flirtatious innuendos, 'I Can See You' sees Taylor addressing a possible lover and their attraction to one another. Co-produced with Antonoff, the song features a guitar riff that gives it an edgier element in comparison to the rest of the album, and overall boasts an experimental sound reminiscent of that explored by Taylor in the albums *reputation* and *Midnights*, while the sexually suggestive lyrics are a reminder of the song 'Dress.' This is currently the only vault track from the album to get a proper music video, which stars Taylor's ex-boyfriend Taylor Lautner.

CASTLES CRUMBLING (FEAT. HAYLEY WILLIAMS)

This is arguably one of the most emotional and introspective songs on the album. 'Castles Crumbling' sees Taylor teaming up with Hayley Williams, a long-time friend and lead vocalist of Paramore. In an interview with *Coup de Main* magazine, Hayley explained that the song is "about an experience that both of us have shared growing up in the public eye". Indeed, the lyrics explore the complexities and pressures of fame, self-doubt and ultimately, Taylor's fear of losing the support of her fans and her career. Another Antonoff co-production, 'Castles Crumbling' is a moody ballad that stands out from the majority of the album, which largely focuses on romantic relationships.

FOOLISH ONE

In this track, co-produced with Dessner, Taylor narrates the pain of unrequited love, the hopeless romantic inside her waiting in vain for the person she loves to return her feelings. The song's melancholic production emphasises the heartbreak of teen love and inexperience, but ultimately ends with Taylor accepting that the person she loves has chosen someone else and realising her foolishness. Since the song's release, it has been heavily speculated that 'Foolish One' is about Taylor's ex, singer John Mayer, although this has not been confirmed. Interestingly, the line "It's delicate" in the second verse ended up becoming an entire song for her 2017 album *reputation*.

TIMELESS

This sentimental ballad explores the idea of fate and enduring love. In the lyrics, Taylor imagines her relationship in different time periods and decides that no matter what, they would have found each other. A country-pop classic that fits in well with the original songs of *Speak Now*, 'Timeless' is backed by a mixture of acoustic guitars, drums and piano, and even includes a nod to *Romeo and Juliet*, the inspiration behind her hit single 'Love Story'. The lyric video for 'Timeless' includes photos of Taylor's grandparents, Marjorie and Robert Finlay, whose relationship likely inspired the song.

LEFT When this re-recording came out, Taylor added 'Long Live' to The Eras Tour setlist after 'Enchanted'.

taylor's version

1989

On the ninth anniversary of the original release, Taylor's best-selling album got its hotly anticipated re-record, and this retro-pop tour de force sounds better than ever

RELEASE DATE 27 OCTOBER 2023

Expectations were sky high for Taylor's fourth re-recorded album, after she announced it was her favourite so far. Back in 2014, the original *1989* cemented Taylor's status as a pop superstar, and it is considered by many critics and fans to be her best album.

Listening to a Taylor's Version is like catching up with an old friend in a new home, and *1989* is no exception. It's comfortable and nostalgic, yet everything feels fresh and more polished. The main album tracks – including iconic chart-topping hits like 'Shake It Off', 'Blank Space' and 'Bad Blood' – still shine as brightly as they did before. Subtle production changes elevate the songs to new heights, without being so different as to be distracting or jarring.

As usual, Taylor does a superb job in recreating her original vocals, while throwing in new flourishes in her delivery here and there. Those little twists always feel natural; never just changes for the sake of it. Her lower register has also grown stronger over the years, providing her with extra power and control in sections like the verses of 'New Romantics', for example.

Some fans were hoping for more 'From the Vault' tracks on this edition, given that over 100 songs were reportedly written for the original album back in 2014. But Taylor has previously spoken about how brutal she had to be when curating the original tracklist: "There were so many songs I wrote for this album that were really good, but if I felt in any way that they would have belonged on my last album, *Red*, they got cut," she explained in a 2015 interview on *The Todd Show in the Morning*. It stands to reason that she may have taken the same approach when deciding on the Vault tracks, to ensure they fit in with her vision for the record as a whole. So we greedy Swifties may have 'only' five new songs, but rest assured they're absolute synth-pop belters.

"SLUT!"

The announcement of this track's name raised a few eyebrows. Some speculated it would be anthemic, perhaps similar to 'ME!', given the exclamation point. But in stark contrast to its punctuation, this track is actually a dreamy, sultry number that addresses the slut shaming Taylor has faced in her high-profile dating life. It describes a relationship that she feels is worth pursuing despite all the unfair scrutiny that falls on her, highlighting the double standards that female public figures face in their relationships ("I'll pay the price, you won't"). Despite the song's gentle vocals, it also sends a defiant message – Taylor will date whoever she wants, and the right partner makes it easier to shrug off the incessant media commentary: "If they call me a 'slut', you know it might be worth it for once".

SAY DON'T GO

On this track, Taylor collaborated with songwriting legend Dianne Warren, who has hits like 'How Do I Live' by LeAnn Rimes and Aerosmith's 'I Don't Want to Miss a Thing' among her many credits. The result is a soaring power ballad that wouldn't feel out of place playing as the credits roll on an 80s romantic drama. It explores her coming to terms with an inevitable heartbreak, yet she can't help but hope that her partner will have a change of heart. The relationship is emotionally unbalanced, with Taylor pining while her partner seems distant and disinterested, just dropping the occasional crumbs of affection to keep her hanging on: "'Cause you kiss me and it stops time. And I'm yours, but you're not mine."

NOW THAT WE DON'T TALK

At just two minutes and 26 seconds, this is the shortest song in Taylor's discography so far, but it sure packs a punch as she takes aim at an estranged ex with her weapon of wit. It's a showcase of Taylor's vocal range as she effortlessly moves from the lower notes of the verses up through an ascending scale in the falsetto chorus. Against a backdrop of pulsing, shimmering synths, Taylor deftly skips through the lines "now that – we don't – talk" and the outro with her supremely catchy delivery that makes this an instant favourite. "[This] is one of my favorite songs that was left behind," Taylor explained on Tumblr. "It was so hard to leave it behind, but I think we wrote it a little bit towards the end of the process, and we couldn't get the production right at the time."

SUBURBAN LEGENDS

This song tells the tale of a past relationship between two high-profile figures with a powerful connection. While Taylor initially has a fantasy about how the relationship will go, it ends in disillusionment. At first, she forgave her ex's poorly concealed infidelities ("You had people who called you on unmarked numbers in my peripheral vision"), because she believed they were destined to be together ("We were born to be national treasures"). While the ex continued to string her along, she ultimately decided to end things even though it was painful ("I broke my own heart 'cause you were too polite to do it").

IS IT OVER NOW?

Many songs on *1989* are assumed to be inspired by Taylor's relationship with Harry Styles, but this track is as close to confirmation as we will likely get. It features references to specific incidents that occurred during their time together: "Red blood, white snow" (the snowmobile accident also referenced in 'Out of the Woods') and "Blue dress, on a boat" (a paparazzi photo of Taylor leaving their vacation alone). Against atmospheric synths, Taylor delivers some of her best lyrics, exploring the blurry lines of a breakup. The song also features a middle eight that will immediately join the pantheon of addictive Swift bridges, including the devastating line: "I think about jumping off of very tall somethings, just to see you come running" – instantly iconic.

— ◆ —

LEFT Taylor wore blue versions of some of her Eras Tour outfits on 9 August 2023, to tease the announcement of *1989 (Taylor's Version)*.

TEAM TAYLOR

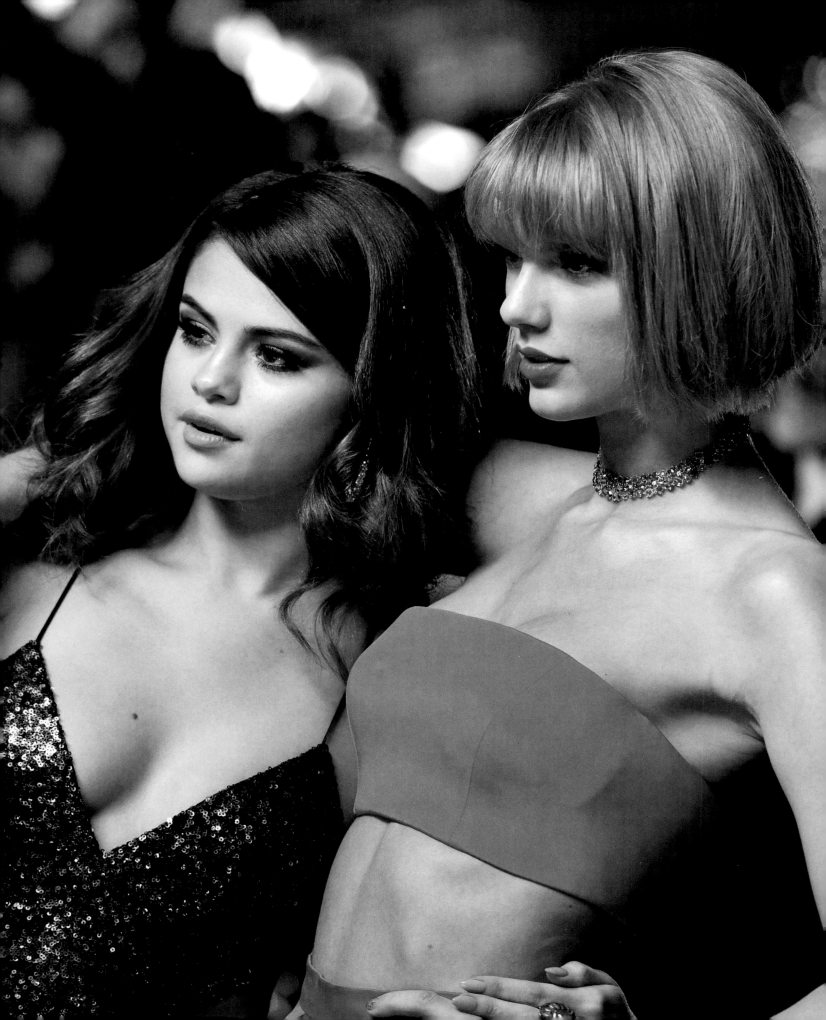

TEAM TAYLOR

From her high-profile romances to her famous friendships and celebrity fall outs, take a deep dive into who's on Team Taylor – and who isn't...

⁕

Taylor wouldn't be the star she is today without her rich network of personal and professional relationships. Her family, friends and collaborators have all supported her throughout her career, while her love life has provided much inspiration for her songwriting over the years. Sadly there are also those who have very publicly brought friction and hostility into Taylor's life, but she has handled every feud and dispute with maturity, conscientiously navigating these problems and becoming all the stronger for it.

TAYLOR'S RELATIONSHIPS

Taylor's dating life has been a central focus of her career, with her honest and raw look at teenage romance being one of the things that drew so many fans to her when she started releasing music. But, as the saying goes, the course of true love never did run smooth, and she has certainly had her fair share of ups and downs.

Taylor is currently in a relationship with American football player Travis Kelce, a tight end for the Kansas City Chiefs. Widely considered to be one of the greatest tight ends in the history of the NFL, Travis has played for the Chiefs for his entire NFL career and has broken several records along the way – for example, in 2022, he became the fastest tight end to reach an incredible 10,000 career yards. He has also won three Super Bowls, including the 2024 game attended by Taylor, which drew a huge audience of football fans and Swifties alike to make it the most watched US TV broadcast since the Moon landing.

With his brother Jason, Travis hosts the hit podcast *New Heights*, where he first revealed to fans in July 2023 that he had tried to introduce himself to Taylor earlier that month, after attending her Eras show in Kansas City. He had made a bracelet for her with his phone number on it, but failed to meet her. "I was disappointed that she doesn't talk before or after her shows because she has to save her voice for the 44 songs that she sings," he explained.

However, by September rumours were swirling that the pair had managed to meet, and that they had hit it off and were dating. Travis remained coy when he was asked about it in interviews, but he confessed on 21 September that "he threw the ball in her court" and had invited her to watch him play. Three days later, Swifties were shocked and delighted when Taylor was spotted cheering on the Kansas City Chiefs during their game against the Chicago Bears. She watched the game from Kelce's suite alongside his mother, Donna, and was later filmed leaving with Kelce in his convertible, all but confirming that they were officially dating. In an interview with *TIME* in December 2023, Taylor confirmed that she was already in a relationship with Kelce by the time she made her first appearance at that NFL game. "We would never be psychotic enough to hard launch a first date," she laughed.

—✦—

RIGHT Taylor with some of her incredible Eras Tour dancers during a show in Atlanta, Georgia, April 2023.

David Eulitt/Getty Images

Since then, the couple have been spotted together on several occasions looking loved up, and they have not shied away from the public and the press as much as Taylor has done in previous relationships. Taylor has attended several of Kelce's games, leading to a surge in interest in the NFL and Kelce himself amongst Swifties, while Kelce has been spotted supporting Taylor during some of her Eras Tour shows. During a show in Argentina, which Kelce attended, Taylor famously changed the lyrics to her song 'Karma', singing "Karma is the guy on the Chiefs, coming straight home to me." Their relationship has seemingly gone from strength to strength, leading to speculation among fans that Taylor has met her match.

Taylor's previous relationship was with British actor Joe Alwyn. The pair had been together since 2016, but had decided to go their separate ways around the start of The Eras Tour in spring 2023. Throughout their relationship,

Taylor and Joe had kept many details of their relationship under wraps, and the end of it was no different – neither have commented on the breakup itself.

After the split, fans and the media were convinced Taylor had briefly been seeing The 1975's Matty Healy. The pair were spotted out and about together following Taylor's breakup with Joe. Again, these rumours were never officially confirmed. Such intense speculation whenever Taylor is seen hanging out with men, even when they are just friends, is something Taylor addressed in her liner notes for *1989 (Taylor's Version)*: "It became clear to me that for me there was no such thing as casual dating. Or even having a male friend who you platonically hang out with," she explained. "If I was seen with him, it was assumed I was sleeping with him."

While they are no longer a couple, Joe was a huge part of Taylor's life. It's likely he and Taylor met at an entertainment industry event. Some fans think 'Dress', from *reputation* might hold some clues. The lyric in question? "Flashback to when you met me, your buzzcut and my hair bleached." Taylor bleached her hair a striking platinum blonde for the 2016 Met Gala and Joe, you guessed it, turned up to the ceremony with his usually mid-length hair in a soldier-short buzzcut, leading some fans to believe that might be where the couple first met.

— ✦ —

ABOVE Photographers at NFL games have managed to capture candid shots of Taylor's unguarded reactions.

LEFT Taylor and Travis' all-American love story has drawn a whole new audience to the NFL. The 2024 Super Bowl became the most watched US television broadcast since the Moon landing in 1969.

"Famous from a young age, Taylor's had to contend with having all of her relationships dissected by fans and the media alike"

— ✦ —

At the time, Taylor was in a relationship with Scottish DJ Calvin Harris, though they reportedly broke up not long after the Gala. After her subsequent relationship with actor Tom Hiddleston came to an end in September 2016, rumours that Joe and Taylor had become an item began to circulate in the media.

Taylor and Joe didn't publicly confirm their relationship for a long time, but they were occasionally spotted at the same events, even if not pictured together. The pair were reportedly at the same Kings of Leon concert after-party in October 2016 and then, a month later, Taylor was seen sneaking into the premiere of Joe's film *Billy Lynn's Long Halftime Walk*. It wasn't until the couple were photographed having coffee together in Nashville the following June that their relationship seemed to be unofficially confirmed.

Taylor had good reason to want to try and keep her growing relationship with Joe on the down-low. Famous from a young age, she's had to contend with having all of her relationships dissected by fans and the media alike. After breaking up with Calvin Harris, she quickly found herself dating Tom Hiddleston just weeks later, something that the public and press leapt on with arguably unfair scrutiny. With Joe, Taylor seemed keen to keep her private life, well, private.

Speaking to *The Guardian* before the release of her seventh album, *Lover*, Taylor spoke about why keeping her relationship with Joe quiet was so important to her. "I've learned that if I do [speak about it], people think it's up for discussion, and our relationship isn't up for discussion," she explained. "If you and I were having a glass of wine right now, we'd be talking about it – but it's just that it goes out into the world. That's where the boundary is, and that's where my life has become manageable. I really want to keep it feeling manageable."

Joe had also spoken, if only briefly, about how much he valued the private side of their relationship. In an interview with *Esquire* from 2018, he was asked if he sought out any guidance from friends when the two of them first started dating. "I didn't seek out advice on that," he replied.

"Because I know what I feel about it. I think there's a very clear line as to what somebody should share, or feel like they have to share, and what they don't want to and shouldn't have to."

The pair also worked together on tracks for Taylor's records *folklore*, *evermore* and *Midnights*, as Joe co-wrote and co-produced several songs for the albums under the pseudonym William Bowery. In a rare public mention of their relationship, when *folklore* won the Album of the Year Grammy in 2021, Taylor thanked Joe in her acceptance speech: "[I want to thank] Joe, who is the first person that I play every single song that I write, and I had the best time writing songs with you in quarantine."

Before Joe, Taylor's approach to her love life had been quite different. As well as singing about her exes in her music, she often spoke publicly about them too. Taylor dated Joe Jonas of the Jonas Brothers between July and October 2008, with things ending when Joe broke up with Taylor via a phone call. "When I find that person that is right for me [...] I'm not even going to be able to remember the boy who broke up with me over the phone in 25 seconds when I was 18," she said on *The Ellen DeGeneres Show* after the split, explaining that the song 'Forever & Always' is about their relationship.

Taylor's 2012 single 'We Are Never Ever Getting Back Together' is rumoured to be about her relationship with actor Jake Gyllenhaal, who she dated between October and December 2010. She calls him out in the song for his 'exhausting' change of heart and musical taste, joking: "You hide away and find your peace of mind with some indie record that's much cooler than mine." She told *Rolling Stone* in 2014 that her song 'Out of the Woods' – widely believed to be about Harry Styles, who she dated from late 2012 until early 2013 – is about a relationship where "every day was a

— ✦ —

RIGHT Swifties love speculating which of Taylor's former partners could have inspired certain songs. From left to right - Jake Gyllenhaal, Calvin Harris and Joe Alwyn.

struggle. Forget making plans for life – we were just trying to make it to next week."

When Taylor and Calvin Harris broke up after a 15-month relationship in June 2016, it seemed she was more than ready to make her future relationships more private. "I went out on a normal amount of dates in my early 20s, and I got absolutely slaughtered for it," she told *Vogue*. "It took a lot of hard work and altering my decision making. I didn't date for two and a half years [before Calvin]. Should I have had to do that? No." She has often criticised the fact that her relationships are often reduced to simply being fodder for internet slideshows.

Besides the constant media attention surrounding her dating life, Taylor has also had to field awkward interview questions about marriage and motherhood. Back in 2019, when a German news outlet asked her – since she was approaching her 30th birthday – if she wanted "to be a mother someday, to have children", Taylor politely refused to entertain the question. "I don't really think men are asked that question when they turn 30," she quite rightly pointed out, "So I'm not going to answer that now."

TAYLOR'S SQUAD

It's not just Taylor's past romances that have drawn attention, but her friendship group too. She moved away from her country music roots and became a bona fide pop artist with the release of her fifth studio album *1989*. With that came the emergence of Taylor's 'girl squad', a group of famous musicians, actresses and models who were regularly seen with her at parties, industry events and celebrating the Fourth of July during Taylor's extravagant yearly bashes at her Rhode Island mansion.

She counted the likes of actors Lena Dunham, Emma Stone and Hailee Steinfeld; models Karlie Kloss, Cara Delevigne and Gigi Hadid; and fellow pop stars Selena Gomez, Lorde, HAIM and Hayley Williams as part of her 'squad', among others. They were regularly seen hanging out on each other's Instagram feeds, with many of them also starring as members of Taylor's all-female fighting force in the music video for her song 'Bad Blood' and appearing on stage during shows for her 1989 World Tour.

Speaking about why she wanted to showcase her new friendship group to the world at that time, Taylor said it

— ✦ —

"She has showed up for me in ways
that I would have never expected.

Flown in because I was hurt and
was going through something.
Stuff that was going on with
my family. It's been proven year
after year and in every moment
of my life that she is one of my
best friends in the world.

We don't agree on everything,
but we respect each other
with everything."

—✦—

SELENA GOMEZ ON HER FRIENDSHIP WITH TAYLOR

RIGHT Selena Gomez and Taylor have been friends for over 15 years,
supporting each other's careers along the way.

"Constantly being in the spotlight means Taylor's disagreements and feuds are often brutally public"

came down to the insecurities she had over not having had many friends growing up. "Even as an adult, I still have recurring flashbacks of sitting at lunch tables alone or hiding in a bathroom stall, or trying to make a new friend and being laughed at," she wrote in a 2019 essay for *ELLE*. "In my twenties I found myself surrounded by girls who wanted to be my friend. So I shouted it from the rooftops, posted pictures and celebrated my newfound acceptance into a sisterhood, without realizing that other people might still feel the way I did when I felt so alone. It's important to address our long-standing issues before we turn into the living embodiment of them."

Over time, the posts celebrating Taylor's sisterhood died down and, although many of them still remain close, other members of Taylor's 'squad' seemed to drift apart. She addressed this in the same essay for *ELLE*, writing about how friendships can shift over time: "Something about 'we're in our young twenties!' hurls people together into groups that can feel like your chosen family. And maybe they will be for the rest of your life. Or maybe they'll just be your comrades for an important phase, but not forever. It's sad but sometimes when you grow, you outgrow relationships. You may leave behind friendships along the way, but you'll always keep the memories."

TAYLOR VS THE WORLD

Constantly being in the spotlight not only means Taylor's romantic relationships and friendships have become well known, but her disagreements and feuds are often brutally public, too.

Her most famous celebrity fall out is probably with rapper Kanye West, with arguments between the two of them dating back over a decade. It began at the 2009 MTV VMA Awards when Taylor, then aged 19, accepted the Best Female Video award for her song 'You Belong With Me', only to find Kanye storm the stage mid-speech and infamously declare "I'mma let you finish" before insisting that Beyoncé should have won instead.

"Yo Taylor, I'm really happy for you, I'mma let you finish, but Beyoncé had one of the best videos of all time!" Kanye

argued as Taylor looked on in confusion. Beyoncé herself looked confused too, while the crowd booed and Taylor reportedly left the stage in tears, having had her moment rudely ruined in front of millions of people.

Although Kanye later apologised, the moment stuck in pop culture history and even President Obama labelled him a 'jackass' over the show-stealing move. Kanye later retracted his apology in 2010, and then again in a 2013 interview with *The New York Times*, saying: "I don't have any regret […] If anyone's reading this waiting for some type of full-on, flat apology for anything, they should just stop reading right now."

Things appeared to be taking a turn for the better a few years later when Kanye and Taylor were pictured at the 2015 Grammys together, and Kanye even spoke of a collaboration with her. Although what he ended up doing next wasn't exactly the kind of collaboration Taylor had in mind…

In February 2016, Kanye released his song 'Famous', which soon became famous for all the wrong reasons after including the line: "I feel like me and Taylor might still have sex. Why? I made that b**** famous." The music video took things a step further, featuring a model of Taylor naked in a giant bed alongside other high-profile pop culture figures and politicians, including Donald Trump, Rihanna and *US Vogue* Editor Anna Wintour.

After the line drew criticism, Kanye took to Twitter to defend himself saying that the line was actually complimentary. "I called Taylor and had an hour long convo with her about the line, and she thought it was funny and gave her blessings," he tweeted, also claiming that the 'b****' lyric was actually Taylor's idea. Taylor responded to this claim via a spokesperson, saying that she didn't know about the lyric in question but had "cautioned him about releasing a song with such a strong misogynistic message".

RIGHT The moment of Kanye's infamous interruption of Taylor's speech at the 2009 MTV VMAs.

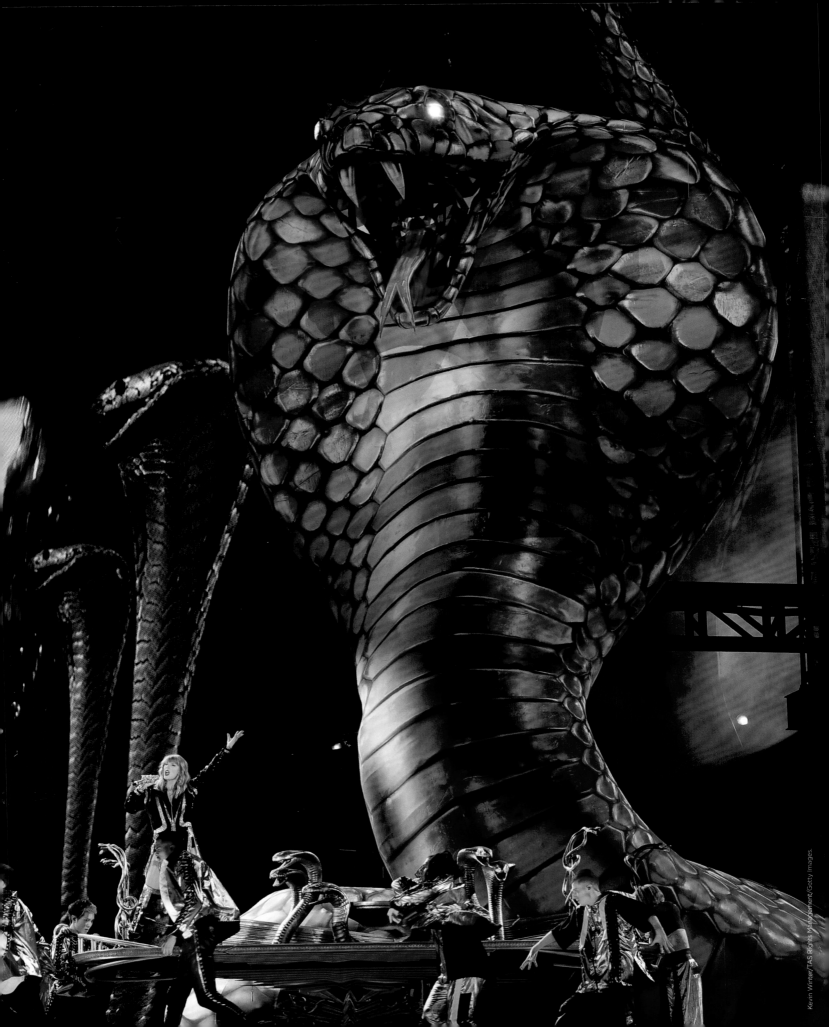

Just a few weeks later, when accepting the Album of the Year Grammy for *1989*, Taylor appeared to take a dig at Kanye claiming he had anything to do with her success. "There are going to be people along the way who try to undercut your success or take credit for your accomplishments or your fame – but if you just focus on the work and you don't let those people sidetrack you, someday when you get where you're going, you'll look around and you will know that it was you, and the people who love you, who put you there – and that will be the greatest feeling in the world," she said in her speech.

But things didn't end there. Kanye's then wife, Kim Kardashian, released footage allegedly showing Kanye speaking to Taylor on a phone call approving the song, posting it to social media captioned with the snake emoji. Taylor responded by saying that, although she had spoken to Kanye, she had never heard or approved 'Famous', claiming Kanye "promised to play the song for me, but he never did". She ended the statement saying: "I would very much like to be excluded from this narrative, one that I have never asked to be a part of, since 2009."

All of this fallout from the past few years – her unfairly scrutinised romantic relationships, the arguments and feuds

with some of the people she thought were her friends, and her anger towards a public she often felt abandoned by – were addressed in Taylor's 2017 album *reputation*. Clearing her Instagram ahead of the album's release, she teased the album announcement with videos of snakes and used the imagery throughout the album campaign, even using a giant snake as part of her stage design for the album's tour. She wanted to take back the narrative of her being 'a snake' into her own hands.

"A few years ago, someone started an online hate campaign by calling me a snake on the internet. The fact that so many people jumped on board with it led me to feeling lower than I've ever felt in my life, but I can't tell you how hard I had to keep from laughing every time my 63-foot inflatable cobra named Karyn appeared on stage

— ✦ —

LEFT Taylor used the 'snake' reference during her Reputation Stadium Tour, performing in front of a giant inflatable serpent, nicknamed Karyn.

BELOW Kanye and Taylor seemed to put their feud behind them at the 2015 MTV VMAs, but it was reignited a few months later when Kanye's 'Famous' was released.

John Shearer/Getty Images.

"Katy sent Taylor a literal olive branch on the opening night of her Reputation Stadium Tour, seemingly as an apology"

in front of 60,000 screaming fans. It's the stadium tour equivalent of responding to a troll's hateful Instagram comment with 'lol'," she explained in *ELLE* in 2019.

In Taylor's comeback after her self-imposed seclusion, *reputation*'s lead single 'Look What You Made Me Do' referenced her feud with Kanye. The accompanying music video featured Taylor wearing her 2009 VMA outfit, poking fun at herself and repeating the line saying that she "would like to be excluded from this narrative".

The dispute made headlines yet again in March 2020 when a recording of the phone call between Kanye and Taylor was leaked online. The recording implied that the clip Kim had previously posted was edited and manipulated, and that Kanye had omitted the term 'b****' when he got Taylor's approval for the line. For Swifties, this was seen as long-overdue vindication for Taylor.

Kanye West isn't the only celebrity that Taylor has had a famous falling out with. She also had a long running feud with Katy Perry, which began in 2014 when Katy allegedly hired some dancers for her Prism Tour directly from Taylor's tour. The rumours that the two were feuding only grew when Taylor started talking about the inspiration for her song 'Bad Blood'. Speaking to *Rolling Stone*, she explained that the track was about "another female artist" that she didn't want to name.

"For years, I was never sure if we were friends or not. She would come up to me at awards shows and say something and walk away, and I would think, 'Are we friends, or did she just give me the harshest insult of my life?'"

Then, the unnamed female pop star crossed a line, Taylor insisted. "She did something so horrible. I was like, 'Oh, we're just straight-up enemies.' And it wasn't even about a guy! It had to do with business. She basically tried to sabotage an entire arena tour. She tried to hire a bunch of people out from under me. And I'm surprisingly non-confrontational – you would not believe how much I hate conflict. So now I have to avoid her. It's awkward, and I don't like it."

In 2017, Katy released 'Swish Swish', a song that some fans think is about Taylor with its lyrics about winning

over someone in a fight: "So keep calm, honey, I'mma stick around, for more than a minute, get used to it. Funny my name keeps comin' out your mouth, 'cause I stay winning."

The following year, though, both singers seemed to have made up when Katy sent Taylor a literal olive branch on the opening night of her Reputation Stadium Tour, seemingly as an apology. And if that wasn't a clear enough sign that their disagreements were all water under the bridge, in 2019 Katy made an appearance in Taylor's music video for 'You Need to Calm Down'. In this case, it seems like time really can heal all wounds.

THE MASTERS DISPUTE

In 2019, Taylor had to contend with perhaps her biggest business battle to be played out publicly so far when Scooter Braun – the music industry heavyweight behind the careers of artists such as Justin Bieber, Ariana Grande, Usher and Kanye West – acquired the masters of her records by buying her former label, Big Machine Label Group, in a deal reported to be worth $300 million.

When Taylor's deal with her first label, Big Machine, came to an end after 12 years in 2018, she had to face the decision of whether to renew the deal or move on to another label. Later that year, she announced she'd signed a multi-album deal with Universal Music Group (UMG) under their label Republic Records. Crucially, her new deal with UMG offered her the chance to own her own master recordings of any albums she made for the label.

A 'master' is basically the final version of a song or album, from which all copies of it – vinyls, CDs, digital downloads, streaming files and so on – are made. In Taylor's original deal with Big Machine, she didn't own the masters for the albums she made for the label, but rather earned a percentage of money from any sales or uses of the song while her record label retained ownership of the

RIGHT Taylor posing for photos with Katy Perry in 2010, several years before their famous fall out.

Kevin Mazur/WireImage/Getty Images

GRAMMY AWARDS | BEVERLY HILLS | 30 JAN 2010

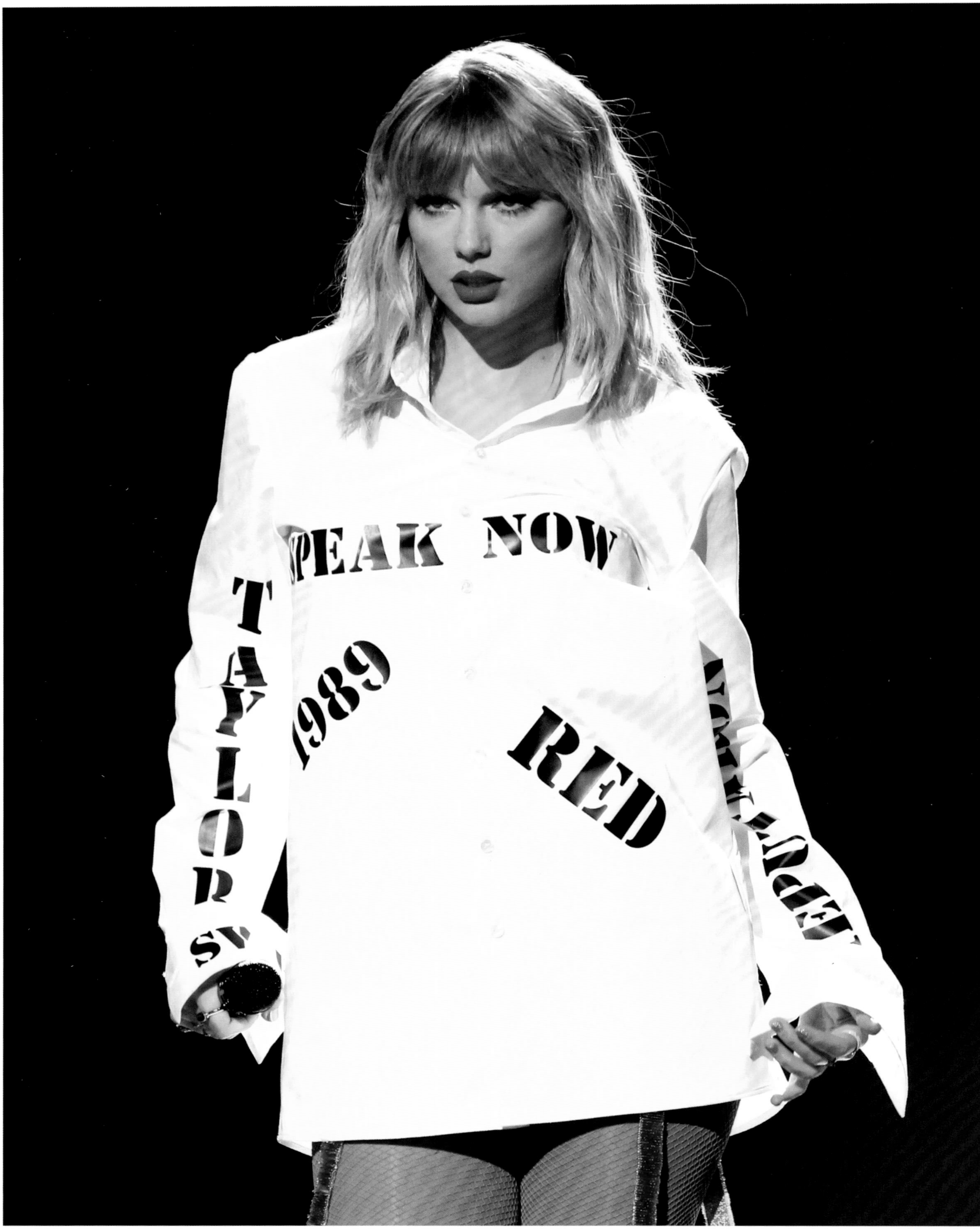

Tommaso Boddi/WireImage/Getty Images.

"Not only has Taylor reclaimed ownership of her songs, she has also raised awareness of the issues surrounding artists' rights"

— ✦ —

original master. This is a fairly common practice in the industry, because record labels want to make sure they have a way to earn back the financial investment they've made in the artist and their music.

Taylor's new deal with UMG offered something slightly different – the right for the label to produce copies of her music to sell, while Taylor still retained the master rights to her work. This crucial difference is great news for Taylor, as it means she'll have more control over her own music. But the masters of her first six albums, from *Taylor Swift* to *reputation*, still belonged to her old label, something which Taylor wasn't happy with when Scooter Braun bought the label and, with it, her life's work.

"When I left my masters in Scott's [the CEO of Big Machine] hands, I made peace with the fact that eventually he would sell them. Never in my worst nightmares did I imagine the buyer would be Scooter," she wrote on Tumblr when news of the sale broke on 30 June 2019. "Any time Scott Borchetta has heard the words 'Scooter Braun' escape my lips, it was when I was either crying or trying not to. He knew what he was doing; they both did. Controlling a woman who didn't want to be associated with them. In perpetuity. That means forever."

Taylor had been trying to buy her master recordings from Big Machine for years, she explained, but Scott Borchetta – "someone for whom the term 'loyalty' is clearly a contractual concept'" Taylor insisted – had refused to budge. After her feud with Kanye, who used to be managed by Braun, this was her worst nightmare.

"All I could think about was the incessant, manipulative bullying I've received at his hands for years," Taylor wrote. "Like when Kim Kardashian orchestrated an illegally recorded snippet of a phone call to be leaked and then Scooter got his two clients together to bully me online about it… Or when his client, Kanye West, organized a revenge porn music video which strips my body naked," she explained. "Now Scooter has stripped me of my life's work, that I wasn't given an opportunity to buy. Essentially, my musical legacy is about to lie in the hands of someone who tried to dismantle it."

Borchetta denied that he had ever stopped Taylor trying to own her masters, writing in a statement on the Big Machine website: "100% of all Taylor Swift assets were to be transferred to her immediately upon signing the new agreement… My offer to Taylor, for the size of our company, was extraordinary. Taylor and I remained on very good terms when she told me she wanted to speak with other record companies and see what was out there for her. I never got in her way and wished her well."

Braun, meanwhile, insisted: "I would like to find a resolution… I'm open to ALL possibilities. My attempts and calls to have an open discussion with you over the last six months have all been rejected. While some on your team and many of our mutual friends have tried to get you to the table, all have had no luck. It almost feels as if you have no interest in ever resolving the conflict."

Taylor responded by saying she'd re-record new versions of her old songs, if necessary, and many celebrities rallied around her in support. Selena Gomez wrote on Instagram: "I can tell you first hand the MOST important thing to Taylor is her family, love, her fans, and her MUSIC. I really hope there is a change of heart over this unfortunate situation." Fans started using the hashtag #IStandWithTaylor on Twitter, which started trending.

After regaining the rights to re-record her back catalogue in November 2020, Taylor didn't waste any time; within a year she had released the new 'Taylor's Versions' of *Fearless* and *Red*. Amid her busy 2023 touring schedule, she released *Speak Now* and *1989*. All the new versions so far have been hugely successful.

Through this project, not only has Taylor reclaimed ownership of her songs, she's also raised awareness of issues surrounding artists' rights. What's more, all the Swifties on Team Taylor have demonstrated to the music industry what a powerful and valuable asset fan loyalty can be.

— ✦ —

LEFT At the 2019 AMAs, Taylor made a statement by taking to the stage in a shirt emblazoned with the titles of her first six albums.

CHAPTER 4

STYLE & SUBSTANCE

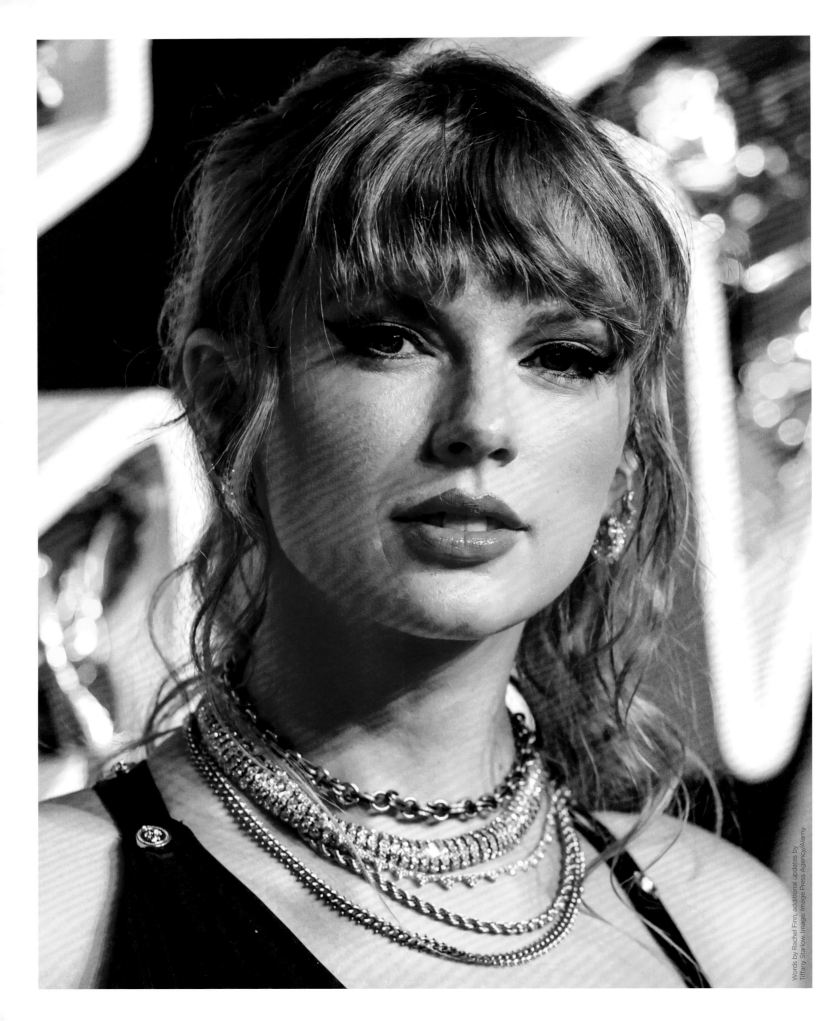

Words by Rachel Finn, additional updates by Tiffany Starlow. Image: Image Press Agency/Alamy

STYLE & SUBSTANCE

In her journey to becoming a global superstar, Taylor has undergone a transformation in so many ways, from her evolving fashion to her growing involvement in activism and social issues

With a career spanning nearly two decades, it's no surprise that Taylor's style has changed over the years. Just like any of us, her fashion sense has evolved and matured since her teenage years. But Taylor's style goes beyond the superficial element of looking good – she has earned a reputation for doing good, too. As one of the most famous and influential people in the world, she has become more confident about standing up for the causes she believes in, using her platform to bring attention to various issues and petition for positive change.

FASHION EVOLUTION

Growing up in the spotlight meant that Taylor's fashion evolution – from teenager, to twenty-something and now as a superstar in her early 30s – was played out for all to see. And as anyone who's ever looked back on their questionable teen fashion choices will be able to tell you, it would be easy to regret some outfits from your younger years – especially when photographic evidence of them exists online!

Taylor, however, seems to take a more laid-back approach. Speaking to *ELLE* magazine in 2015, she talked about how she feels no need to reject any of her former style decisions. "As far as the need to rebel against the idea of you, or the image of you: Like, I feel no need to burn down the house I built by hand," she explained. "I can make additions to it. I can redecorate. But I built this. And so I'm not going to sit there and say, 'Oh, I wish I hadn't had corkscrew-curly hair and worn cowboy boots and sundresses to awards shows when I was 17; I wish I hadn't gone through that fairytale phase where I just wanted to wear princess dresses to awards shows every single time.' Because I made those choices. I did that."

Just as Taylor's music has evolved over the years, so has her fashion. When she first began attending red carpet events around the release of her self-titled debut album in 2006, her style was heavily inspired by a country music aesthetic, wearing her hair in tight curls and regularly donning cowboy boots and long, flowing dresses.

The *Fearless* era took this look further, with Taylor's 2009-2010 stadium tour seeing her wear an array of glamorous princess-inspired gowns (as a nod to the music video for her *Romeo and Juliet*-inspired 'Love Story'), and a marching band costume (inspired by her video for 'You Belong with Me'), a look that also continued through her *Speak Now* era.

—◆—

LEFT Eagle-eyed Swifties examine every detail of Taylor's outfits for potential Easter eggs or hints about upcoming announcements.

Christopher Polk/ACMA2010/Getty Images.

But by the time Taylor got to the release of 2012's *Red*, a move towards a more pop-oriented sound came with a new style. The album's title, predictably, meant Taylor was seen both on-stage and at events in bold scarlet looks with a splash of bright red lipstick, but she also veered into classic, clean-cut styles – high-waisted shorts, blouses, stripy tops and a range of stylish hats. It was perhaps the most relatable and practical era of Taylor's fashion journey so far, moving away from the fairytale-inspired looks of her early career and into something a bit more accessible, yet still fashionable. "Every artist has their set of priorities," she told *The Guardian* in 2014. "Being looked at as sexy? Not really on my radar. But nice? I really hope that that is the impression."

If *Red* saw Taylor's style encapsulating a brand of stylish, casual sleek, then *1989* took things in a more glamorous direction again. On her world tour for the album, she wore showgirl-themed designs, complete with sequinned playsuits, crop tops, A-Line skirts and some killer heels. A few years later during her Reputation Stadium Tour, she played on the album's dark aesthetic, with black sequinned and snake-print bodysuits and knee-high boots.

One of Taylor's most talked about fashion moments to date was her 2016 Met Gala look. Taylor wore a futuristic silver-panel dress matched with choppy, platinum blonde hair and a deep purple lipstick. On the red carpet, she described herself as a "futuristic gladiator robot" and it was perhaps the most rock 'n' roll look she'd sported to date – and one she carried on for a few months afterwards. She was almost unrecognisable when she appeared on the cover of *Vogue* in May 2016 in sky-high platform boots, a bleach-blonde bob and a glittery slip dress. It was miles away from the girly, country look she was first known for a decade earlier, but Taylor admitted a few years later in an essay she wrote for *ELLE* in 2019, that she wasn't a fan of her brief journey into the style. "If you don't look back at pictures of some of your old looks and cringe, you're doing it wrong," she wrote. "See: Bleachella."

For her seventh album, *Lover*, Taylor's look took inspiration from the rainbow; both her on- and off-stage outfits became softer and lighter, relying heavily on colour and pastels. In comparison to the dark, gothic looks of her *reputation* era, it signalled the biggest change so far for

— ✦ —

ABOVE Taylor's early style was heavily influenced by her country music roots, often performing in cowboy-style boots.

RIGHT Her *Red* era looks always featured the titular colour; she even got a customised guitar complete with hundreds of red crystals.

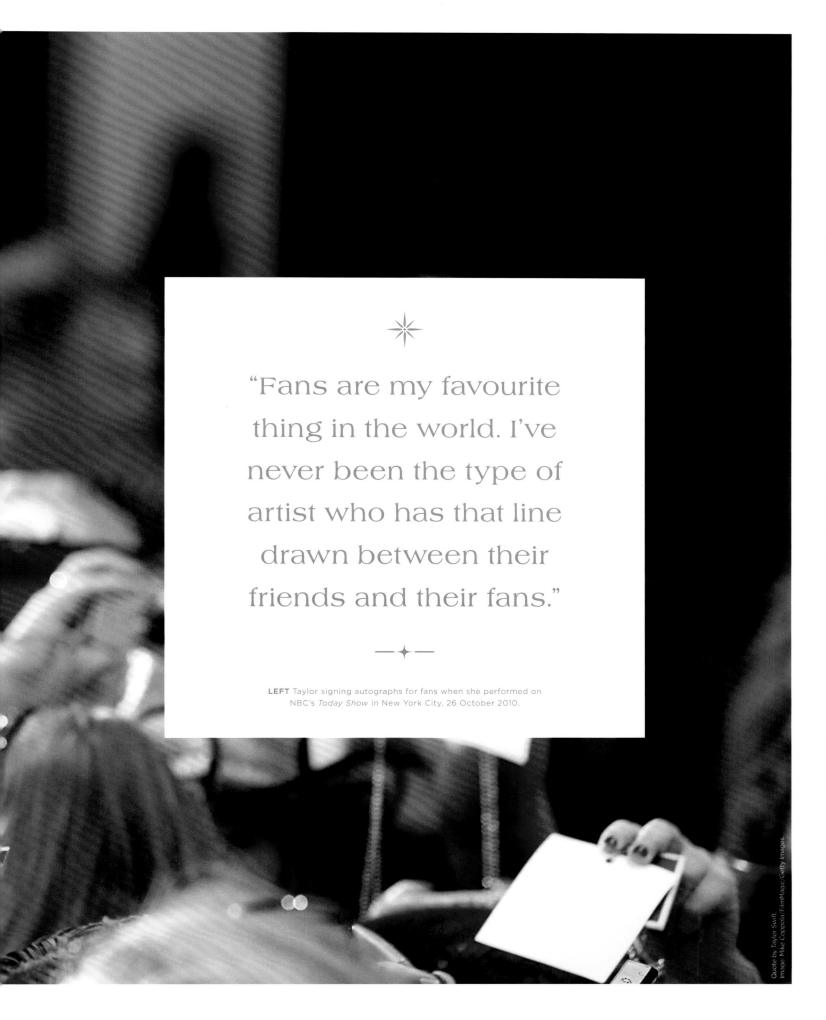

"Fans are my favourite thing in the world. I've never been the type of artist who has that line drawn between their friends and their fans."

LEFT Taylor signing autographs for fans when she performed on NBC's *Today Show* in New York City, 26 October 2010.

Taylor aesthetically between albums, one she announced by posting a number of cryptic clues on her Instagram – posts that all featured butterflies in some way – in the run up to the album announcement itself. If *reputation* played on the idea that Taylor was 'a snake', then it looked like *Lover* was set to be where she spread her wings and flew away from all the drama.

When Taylor surprised the world with her two lockdown albums in 2020, *folklore* and *evermore*, her new indie-folk sound was complemented by relaxed cottagecore and ethereal 'witchy' styles. Where *Lover* was rainbows, these folky sister albums were muted, natural shades, and Taylor embraced cosy knitwear, floaty dresses and low-maintenance hair and makeup.

Coming out of the pandemic lockdowns, and with the release of *Midnights* in 2022, Taylor's style continued to evolve. In recent years, she has introduced some more workwear-inspired looks, such as tailored blazers and chic suits, but she continues to mix things up by incorporating her go-to favourite styles, like cropped tops, bodycon dresses and classic gowns. On the career-spanning Eras Tour, she celebrates not just her music, but also her many different outfits and styles from across the years. Top

fashion designers such as Oscar de la Renta, Roberto Cavalli, Alberta Ferretti and Nicole + Felicia (among others) produced Taylor's stunning on-stage ensembles, featuring throwbacks to her most iconic looks.

SYMBOLS AND CLUES

Taylor has long been a fan of creating a rich world for her fans full of clues, symbols and Easter eggs that link her musical worlds together. 'ME!' was the first music video released for *Lover* and it came full of hints to what fans could expect from the rest of the album. The star-studded video featured Big Ben hidden in the horizon of one of the shots (a nod towards album track 'London Boy'), Ellen DeGeneres getting a tattoo that spelled out 'Cruel Summer' on her forearm (based on the album track of the same name) and singer Hayley Kiyoko shooting an arrow

— ✦ —

RIGHT Over the past few years, Taylor has added more workwear-inspired looks to her wardrobe, with elegant suits and fitted blazers.

BELOW Taylor's striking outfit for the 2016 Met Gala. She would later jokingly refer to this look as 'Bleachella'.

Mike Coppola/People.com/Getty Images.

John Shearer/Getty Images.

MTV VIDEO MUSIC AWARDS | NEW JERSEY | 26 AUG 2019

*"In her early career, much of Taylor's success
came from her connection to her fans"*

into a bullseye that read '5' (a reference to track five: 'The Archer'), among others.

Taylor later released the video for *Lover*'s fourth single, 'The Man', which marked her solo directorial debut. She was unrecognisable in the satirical video, having been transformed by prosthetics and makeup to play the role of sleazy businessman 'Tyler Swift'. It was filled with Easter eggs from Taylor's personal life, including a scene shot in 13th Street Station, a nod to her favourite number. In reference to her dispute with music manager Scooter Braun (over his acquisition of her former record label and, with it, the masters of her first six albums), there's a 'no scooters allowed' sign visible in the subway station. Next to it, there's another that reads 'MISSING – please return to Taylor Swift', alluding to the fact that she was still fighting to get the rights to her own music.

Previous videos of Taylor's have been full of nods towards her earlier life and career experiences too. In the 2017 video for 'Look What You Made Me Do', Taylor is seen bathing in a bathtub full of jewellery and next to her is a one-dollar bill – a reference to the symbolic $1 Taylor successfully counter-sued former radio DJ David Mueller for during the sexual assault case in 2016. It also features her addressing an army of models – poking fun at those who criticised her 'squad' for being all tall, thin and look-alike. When she crashes a car and is surrounded by paparazzi, she has a hair-style suspiciously similar to Katy Perry's and holds up a Grammy – supposedly joking that Katy has yet to win one. "I love to communicate through Easter eggs. I think the best messages are cryptic ones," she told *Entertainment Weekly* in 2019.

TAYLOR'S BOND WITH HER FANS

All these interlinking messages are fun, of course, but they're also part of Taylor's dedication to her fans and wanting to create a visual and conceptual world that goes beyond just the music. In her early career, much of Taylor's success came from her connection to her fans and the fact that she proved that, rather than just being a genre for adults, country music had an untapped market – teenage

girls. Despite not knowing her personally, Taylor's direct and honest lyrics, speaking of heartbreak and unrequited love, mirrored what so many fans would have been going through in their own lives. Rather than dismissing teenage emotions as trivial or overdramatic, she gave them a voice – often because, as a teenager, she was going through the same things that they were too.

"Fans are my favourite thing in the world," she said of her relationship to the Swifties. "I've never been the type of artist who has that line drawn between their friends and their fans. The line's always been really blurred for me. I'll hang out with them after the show. I'll hang out with them before the show. If I see them in the mall, I'll stand there and talk to them for 10 minutes."

Aside from hanging out with fans in real life after shows, their relationship also extends online. Taylor joined Tumblr in 2014, sending Swifties thoughtful messages when they were heartbroken, reblogging their funny memes and liking their posts to confirm or deny their theories about albums. She's also sent fans gifts, and money to help them pay off student loans or help them out of financial difficulty.

An example of Taylor's impromptu charity made headlines in August 2020, when she donated £23,000 (around $30,000) to Vitoria Mario, a young student in London. Vitoria had moved to the UK from Portugal and was struggling to raise the money she needed to study mathematics at university, since she was not eligible for student loans or grants. She had raised about half of her target amount, when Taylor found her page and wrote the message: "Vitoria, I came across your story online and am so inspired by your drive and dedication to turning your dreams into reality. I want to gift you the rest of your goal amount. Good luck with everything you do! Love, Taylor." Vitoria herself was "over the moon" upon seeing the donation: "She actually made my dream come true."

— ✦ —

LEFT Taylor is known to be generous with her time on the red carpet, meeting fans, signing autographs and posing for photos.

"Taylor's music has helped so many of her fans through some of life's most difficult moments"

In a 2012 YouTube video, Taylor explained why she thinks it's so important to give back: "It's honestly one of the most amazing feelings knowing that there's this group of people that has my back, and that they always show up. I try to figure out ways all the time to thank them for that."

Taylor's music has no doubt helped so many of her fans through some of life's most difficult moments, but in turn they've also never hesitated to rally around her in times of crisis. In a plea posted to Twitter after Scooter Braun acquired her old masters in 2019, she wrote: "This is where I'm asking for your help. Please let Scott Borchetta and Scooter Braun know how you feel about this." Fans mobilised with the hashtag #IStandWithTaylor and sent thousands of messages to Borchetta and Braun, asking them to be fair to her in their disagreement.

Not all of Taylor's fans are, well, human though. It's no secret that Taylor is a cat lady (and we mean that as a compliment!) She has three cats: Meredith Grey, Olivia Benson and Benjamin Button. The first to be added to Taylor's feline family in 2011 was Scottish fold Meredith, named after the lead in *Grey's Anatomy*, one of her favourite shows. In 2014, she got second Scottish fold Olivia, named after the protagonist of *Law & Order: SVU*. In 2019, she adopted Ragdoll kitten Benjamin, named after the titular character of *The Curious Case of Benjamin Button* by F Scott Fitzgerald. "They can say whatever they want about my personal life because I know what my personal life is, and it involves a lot of TV and cats and girlfriends," she joked in an interview with *The Guardian* in 2014.

ACTIVISM

Although Taylor first shot to fame writing about her personal life and keeping her career mostly about her music, as she got older, she began to turn her view outwards, speaking out on many political issues that she'd previously been reluctant to talk about. Although this wasn't until she'd gone through a period where she felt under more and more pressure to speak out.

Unlike many celebrities, Taylor didn't explicitly endorse a candidate for the 2016 US presidential election, leading many to believe that, at best, she didn't really care or, at worst, she was actually a secret supporter of right-wing Republican candidate Donald Trump. As the run-up to the election was underway, Taylor seemed busy doing other things, posting pictures of herself on Instagram attending New York Fashion Week, posing with Drake, cuddling koalas and even partying with her celebrity friends waving an American flag at one of her 4th of July parties – all while keeping quiet about any political opinions one way or the other. Some fans assumed that she was keeping quiet due to fears of alienating parts of her fanbase, something which may have happened considering her background in country music, a genre which has historically been popular with many Southern conservative voters. She didn't mention the election publicly at all until the day itself, when she posted a photo of herself queuing to vote with the caption: "Today is the day. Go out and VOTE."

Then it all changed. A few years later, Taylor spoke of her regret of not being more openly political and how, going forward, she wanted to speak out for things she thought were right. In conversation with *The Guardian* in 2019, she explained: "The things that happen to you in your life are what develop your political opinions. I was living in this Obama eight-year paradise of, you go, you cast your vote, the person you vote for wins, everyone's happy! This whole thing, the last three, four years, it completely blindsided a lot of us, me included."

She was also hesitant to speak publicly about social or political issues in the past due to concerns from her previous label. "Throughout my career, label executives would say 'a nice girl doesn't force her opinions on anyone'," she explained in the *Miss Americana* documentary, adding "I feel really, really good about not being muzzled anymore, and it was my own doing."

RIGHT Taylor at the Robert F Kennedy Center for the 2012 Justice and Human Rights Ripple of Hope gala with activist Kerry Kennedy, philanthropist Vincent A Mai and LGBTQ+ advocate Frank Mugisha.

"I enjoyed being able to help her realise that using her voice is a humongous instrument that is able to change the minds of those who, without her, may have never looked at gay people as actual people."

TODRICK HALL ON HIS FRIENDSHIP WITH TAYLOR

LEFT Taylor and Todrick Hall backstage at the Broadway
production of *Kinky Boots* in 2016.

PEOPLE THROW ROCKS
AT THINGS THAT
SHINE

#BlankSpaceForTaylor

Theo Stroomer/Getty Images.

When her next chance to vote came around, this time she didn't keep quiet. She posted to Instagram to endorse the Democratic candidate Phil Bredesen from her home state of Tennessee for the 2018 senate race. This caused a surge in people registering to vote, with more than 65,000 new registrations in the 24 hours following her post – an effect the media called the 'Swift Lift'. Donald Trump's response? "Let's say that I like Taylor's music about 25% less now."

"I hate to admit this, but I felt that I wasn't educated enough on it," she later explained. "Because I hadn't actively tried to learn about politics in a way that I felt was necessary for me, making statements that go out to hundreds of millions of people."

But these days Taylor is older and wiser, and things have changed. In the run up to the 2020 presidential election, she made her political allegiances crystal clear and continues to encourage people to make sure they vote. Responding to Trump's attempts to undermine the postal voting system (with record numbers expected to vote by mail during the ongoing Covid-19 pandemic), she took to Twitter: "Trump's calculated dismantling of USPS proves one thing clearly: He is WELL AWARE that we do not want him as our president. He's chosen to blatantly cheat and put millions of Americans' lives at risk in an effort to hold on to power." Following up with: "Donald Trump's ineffective leadership gravely worsened the crisis that we are in and he is now

taking advantage of it to subvert and destroy our right to vote and vote safely. Request a ballot early. Vote early." It's clear to see that Taylor is no longer holding back!

Voting isn't the only area Taylor has been speaking out about more in recent years. She first made a call for gun control in March 2018, donating an undisclosed amount of money for the March For Our Lives Rally, a student-led movement against gun violence that was founded by survivors of the Stoneman Douglas High School shooting. "No one should have to go to school in fear of gun violence. Or to a nightclub. Or to a concert. Or to a movie theater. Or to their place of worship," Taylor wrote in an Instagram post. The rally's turnout was estimated to be between 1.2-2 million people, making it one of the largest protests in American history. "I've made a donation to show my support for the students, for the March For Our Lives campaign, for everyone affected by these tragedies, and to support gun reform," she added.

— ✦ —

ABOVE Taylor's fans displayed messages of support in the windows of a building across the street during her court case against David Mueller in 2017.

LEFT Shortly after breaking her political silence in an Instagram post, Taylor used her acceptance speech at the 2018 AMAs to encourage people to vote in the US midterm elections.

"Millions of people look up to her... What Taylor says and does matters"

In 2017, after she went to court to defend herself against radio DJ David Mueller – who was fired from his job after groping Taylor during a meet-and-greet in 2013 – she also found herself in the midst of another important social and political movement. Not long after, in October 2017 the hashtag #MeToo went viral, with millions of people around the world – predominantly women – sharing their experiences of sexual harassment and assault, following the multitude of abuse allegations against the now disgraced film producer Harvey Weinstein. Taylor's story became one of many discussed in the movement, with *TIME* magazine including her in their Person of the Year 2017 special as one of the 'Silence Breakers', which documented a range of people across different industries and backgrounds who had spoken out against harassment and assault. "I think that this moment is important for awareness, for how parents are talking to their children, and how victims are processing their trauma, whether it be new or old," Taylor explained in an Instagram post. "The brave women and men who have come forward this year have all moved the needle in terms of letting people know that this abuse of power shouldn't be tolerated."

Taylor has also been outspoken on LGBTQ+ discrimination, something she addresses directly in her single 'You Need to Calm Down' from *Lover*, with the lyrics: "You just need to take several seats and then try to restore the peace, and control your urges to scream about all the people you hate, 'cause shade never made anybody less gay." She also created a petition in support of the Equality Act that she shared at the end of the song's star-studded video. Over 800,000 people signed the petition, and the Equality Act was eventually reintroduced under the Biden administration. As of February 2024, the bill is currently awaiting Senate consideration.

What's more, thanks to the lyric "Why are you mad? When you could be GLAAD?", the release of the song also led to a rise in donations to GLAAD, a non-profit media watchdog advocating for fair and inclusive representation of LGBTQ+ people. Many fans gave symbolic donations of $13, in reference to Taylor's lucky number.

Although Taylor has been more outspoken about LGBTQ+ rights in more recent years, she's spoken about regretting that she hadn't done more in the past. "Maybe a year or two ago, [my friend] Todrick [Hall] and I are in the car, and he asked me, 'What would you do if your son was gay?'" she told *Vogue* in 2019. "The fact that he had to ask me... shocked me and made me realize that I had not made my position clear enough or loud enough. If my son was gay, he'd be gay. I don't understand the question." She added, "If he was thinking that, I can't imagine what my fans in the LGBTQ+ community might be thinking. It was kind of devastating to realise that I hadn't been publicly clear about that."

In June 2020, when global protests broke out after the death of George Floyd, a Black man from Minneapolis who was wrongfully killed by a police officer, Taylor used her platform to speak out about lack of police accountability over racist behaviour. "Racial injustice has been ingrained deeply into local and state governments, and changes must be made there. In order for policies to change, we need to elect people who will fight against police brutality and racism of any kind," she tweeted alongside the Black Lives Matter hashtag. In a tweet to Donald Trump, she added: "After stoking the fires of white supremacy and racism your entire presidency, you have the nerve to feign moral superiority before threatening violence? We will vote you out in November."

Taylor's journey from the girl who won over fans with her honest accounts of teenage life, to this global superstar advocating for some of the most important social issues demonstrates her growing influence. But it also reminds us of the importance of standing up for what's right, even when it doesn't affect us directly. As Taylor summed up to *Vogue* in 2019: "I didn't realise until recently that I could advocate for a community that I'm not a part of."

RIGHT 'You Need to Calm Down' won the Video for Good award – for videos with a social and/or political message – at the 2019 MTV VMAs.

John Shearer/Getty Images.

MTV VIDEO MUSIC AWARDS | NEW JERSEY | 26 AUG 2019

AN ICONIC ROLE MODEL

In short, Taylor is much more than a fashion icon, she has become a wonderful role model for her fans all around the world. Growing up in the public eye is not easy, but she handled her early career and the intense pressures of fame with astonishing maturity and wisdom. Through it all, Taylor has managed to maintain that relatable, down-to-earth attitude that made audiences fall in love with her in the first place.

Even after all these years, her unique bond with her fans is stronger than ever, and has remained an integral part of her unstoppable success. At the premiere for *Taylor Swift: The Eras Tour* concert film, Taylor told fans in the audience, "I think you'll see that you're absolutely a main character in the film. Because it was your magic, and your attention to detail, and your sense of humor, and the ways that you lean into what I'm doing and the music I create, that made this tour the most fun thing I've ever been a part of in my life!"

For a certain generation, we feel as though we have grown up alongside Taylor; she's provided the soundtrack to our most memorable moments – from falling in love to heartbreak, through loneliness and joy – as though she's been there with us through it all, giving voice to every wonderful and chaotic emotion. It's this powerful connection with her millions of fans that makes Taylor one of the most influential people in the world.

And with that power comes great responsibility. The fact is that millions of people look up to her, particularly young girls. What Taylor says and does matters to people, and her actions can have a remarkable impact. No longer hesitant about speaking her mind, she has used the wide-reaching platform of her global fame to become a vocal activist, raising awareness of many social and political issues, and encouraging her fans to vote, sign petitions or make donations where they can.

Taylor also leads by example, with a well-earned reputation of being one of the most generous celebrities when it comes to giving back. Whether it's surprise contributions to Swifties in need of financial assistance, making donations to food banks in the cities she visits on tour, or giving incredibly generous bonus payments to workers, Taylor never hesitates to provide support where she can. And that wonderful spirit of kindness and generosity never goes out of style.

— ✦ —

LEFT Taylor surprised her delighted fans at *The Eras Tour* concert film premiere, as it was never confirmed that she would be able to attend.

CHAPTER 5
SUPERSTAR

SUPERSTAR

All Taylor's successes have made her one of the most influential pop culture icons in the world – and her star is shining brighter than ever

Taylor is without a doubt one of the most famous people on the planet right now. With The Eras Tour, it feels as though we are witnessing a star at the peak of her power. Having more awards than anyone has shelf space for, millions of devoted Swifties cheering her on and even university courses dedicated to her work, Taylor's career so far has truly been historic.

AWARD WINNER

During her career, Taylor has racked up a truly astonishing number of accolades, having won over 650 awards so far and been nominated for 1,250 others. As of February 2024, she has won 14 Grammys, and became the first artist in history to have won the coveted Album of the Year Grammy four times (for *Fearless*, *1989*, *folklore* and *Midnights*). She's also received the prestigious BRITs Global Icon award, 23 MTV Video Music Awards, a record-breaking 40 American Music Awards, plus an Emmy for her concert film *AMEX Unstaged: Taylor Swift Experience* in 2015. That's not forgetting 40 *Billboard* Music Awards, 20 People's Choice Awards, three NME awards, 26 Teen Choice Awards, eight Academy of Country Music Awards, and many, *many* more.

If that wasn't enough, Taylor's broken over 100 Guinness World Records, including chart milestones like 'Most consecutive No.1 studio albums on the US *Billboard* 200' and 'Most US singles chart entries' for a female solo artist. She dominates streaming records, too. In 2022, the release of *Midnights* broke the record for 'Most day-one streams of

an album on Spotify' by a female artist. In November 2023, Taylor briefly overtook The Weeknd to nab the record for 'Most monthly listeners on Spotify', with over 109 million.

In 2019, Taylor's long list of achievements culminated in two major awards, celebrating Taylor's first full decade in music. She was named Artist of the Decade at the American Music Awards as well as *Billboard*'s Woman of the Decade. For the latter, Taylor used her acceptance speech to give a passionate talk about the struggles and successes she's faced in the industry, as well as talking about the importance of nurturing and looking after the younger female pop stars who will come after her.

"In the last ten years I have watched as women in this industry are criticised and measured up to each other and picked at for their bodies, their romantic lives, their fashion…" she said. "Have you ever heard someone say that about a male artist? 'I really like his songs but I don't know what it is, there's just something about him I don't like?' No! That criticism is reserved for us!"

"It seems like the pressure that could have crushed us made us into diamonds instead," she continued. "And what didn't kill us actually did make us stronger. But we need to keep advocating for women in the recording studios, behind the mixing board, in A&R meetings, because rather than

RIGHT Taylor performing a sensational medley of her hits at the American Music Awards in November 2019.

fighting to be taken seriously in their fields, these women are still struggling to even have a chance to be in the room."

In the speech, she also spoke about the intense pressure she's faced from the public and the media and how difficult it can be to meet the impossible standards placed on women in the public eye. "They're saying I'm dating too much in my 20s? Okay, I'll stop, I'll just be single. For years. Now they're saying my album *Red* is filled with too many breakup songs? Okay, I'll make one about moving to New York and deciding that really my life is more fun with just my friends. Oh, they're saying my music is changing too much for me to stay in country music? All right. Okay, here's an entire genre shift and a pop album called *1989*. Now it's that I'm showing you too many pictures of me with my friends, okay, I can stop doing that too. Now I'm actually a calculated manipulator rather than a smart businesswoman? Okay, I'll disappear from public view for years. Now I'm being cast as a villain to you? Okay, here's an album called *reputation* and there are lots of snakes everywhere."

HITTING THE BIG SCREEN

As well as her music, Taylor has also ventured into acting, appearing in several TV shows and films throughout her career. Her first role was in a 2009 episode of *CSI*, where she played Hayley Jones, a rebellious teenager who is killed in suspicious circumstances. She dyes her hair various dark shades, has a lip piercing and a drug-dealing boyfriend – quite the opposite of Taylor in real life!

CSI may have been Taylor's small-screen debut, but she made her first feature film appearance in 2010's *Valentine's Day*, a romantic comedy following a group of interlinking people and their struggles with love on one February 14th. Taylor plays Felicia, the annoying and over-enthusiastic high school girlfriend of William, as they navigate their first-ever relationship. William was played by Taylor's ex-boyfriend Taylor Lautner (fans dubbed them 'Taylor squared') and they first met on set. They dated for a few months while making the film in 2009, but had split up by the time it came out the following year. Taylor (Lautner, that is) later admitted that the song 'Back to December' was about their relationship. "He's one of my best friends," Taylor (Swift) explained to *Glamour* in 2011 when discussing their shared history. "He's wonderful, and we'll always be close. I'm so thankful for that."

— ✦ —

RIGHT Taylor walking the red carpet at the 2023 Grammy Awards.

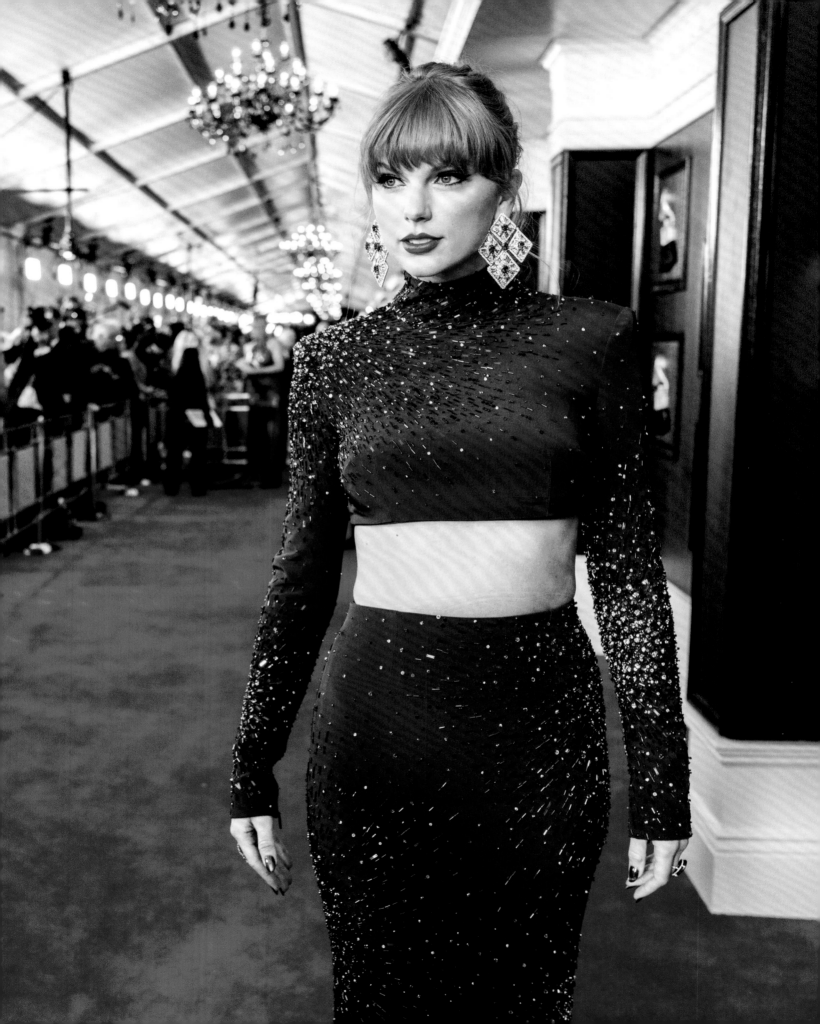

CATS PREMIERE | NEW YORK CITY | 16 DEC 2019

UPI/Alamy Live News.

"Taylor has also leveraged her power to speak out about the struggles of those who work in the music industry"

In 2012, Taylor tried her hand at voice acting in *The Lorax*, playing Audrey in the adaptation of the Dr Seuss classic. Unlike her live music performances or previous acting roles, the film saw Taylor face the challenge of voicing an animated character for the first time. "It's a completely different space that you go to in your head," she explained. "It's very different from when you're singing songs that you wrote. With this, you're sitting there in a booth by yourself having conversations with no one."

Perhaps Taylor's most discussed role to date though is her appearance in *Cats*. The on-screen adaptation of the Sir Andrew Lloyd Webber musical included a star-studded cast alongside Taylor, with appearances from James Corden, Judi Dench, Jason Derulo, Idris Elba, Rebel Wilson and more, with Taylor playing the role of Bombalurina. As a self-confessed cat lady, we can only assume Taylor jumped at the chance to be transformed into feline form through CGI. Her character's big moment comes towards the end of the film when she sings the song 'Macavity' from the musical in a British accent, before sprinkling catnip all over the other cats. And that's about it!

Her screen-time in the actual film may only stretch to a few minutes, but Taylor was more involved behind the scenes, teaming up with Sir Andrew Lloyd Webber to write a new song for the production called 'Beautiful Ghosts'. It's sung in the film by the main character, Victoria, who's played by ballet dancer Francesca Hayward. Judi Dench's character Old Deuteronomy also performs a scaled-back rendition of the song later in the film, while we hear Taylor's full version over the credits. According to Taylor, the song is about trying to find a sense of belonging: "'Beautiful Ghosts' is sung from a young voice who is wondering if she will ever have glory days. Longing for the sense of belonging she sees everyone finding. Reaching for it, desperately afraid of never having beautiful ghosts of days gone by to cling to in her older years."

While the film itself was a commercial and critical flop, Taylor said she just loved the experience of working on it. "I had a really great time working on that weird-ass movie," she told *Variety*. "I'm not gonna retroactively decide that it

wasn't the best experience. I never would have met Andrew Lloyd Webber or gotten to see how he works, and now he's my buddy. I got to work with the sickest dancers and performers. No complaints."

While Taylor has undertaken a range of acting roles over the years, it's clear music is still her one true love and she'll only go for roles she really connects with, rather than doing it just for fame or money (arguably she's got enough of both already anyway!) "When I look at acting careers that I really admire, I see that it's been a precise decision-making process for these people," she explained. "They make decisions based on what they love, and they do only the things that they are passionate about. They play only characters that they can't stop thinking about."

Besides her forays into acting, Taylor has also proven herself to be very talented behind the camera as a director, overseeing many of her own music videos in recent years. She also directed *All Too Well: The Short Film* in 2021, which earned her multiple awards and critical acclaim.

POWER IN THE MUSIC INDUSTRY

As well as using her influence to speak out about political and social issues over the past few years, Taylor has also leveraged her power to speak out about the struggles of those who work in the music industry – particularly artists – in a bid to pave the way for younger and less experienced creatives entering the industry after her.

She famously had a 'boycott' of Spotify between 2014 and 2017, pulling her albums from the streaming service to make a stand against what she said was unfair payment to music creators. Explaining the decision to Yahoo!, Taylor said: "All I can say is that music is changing so quickly, and the landscape of the music industry itself is changing so quickly, that everything new, like Spotify,

LEFT Taylor pictured at the *Cats* world premiere in New York. She also wrote the song 'Beautiful Ghosts' for the film along with musical legend, Sir Andrew Lloyd Webber.

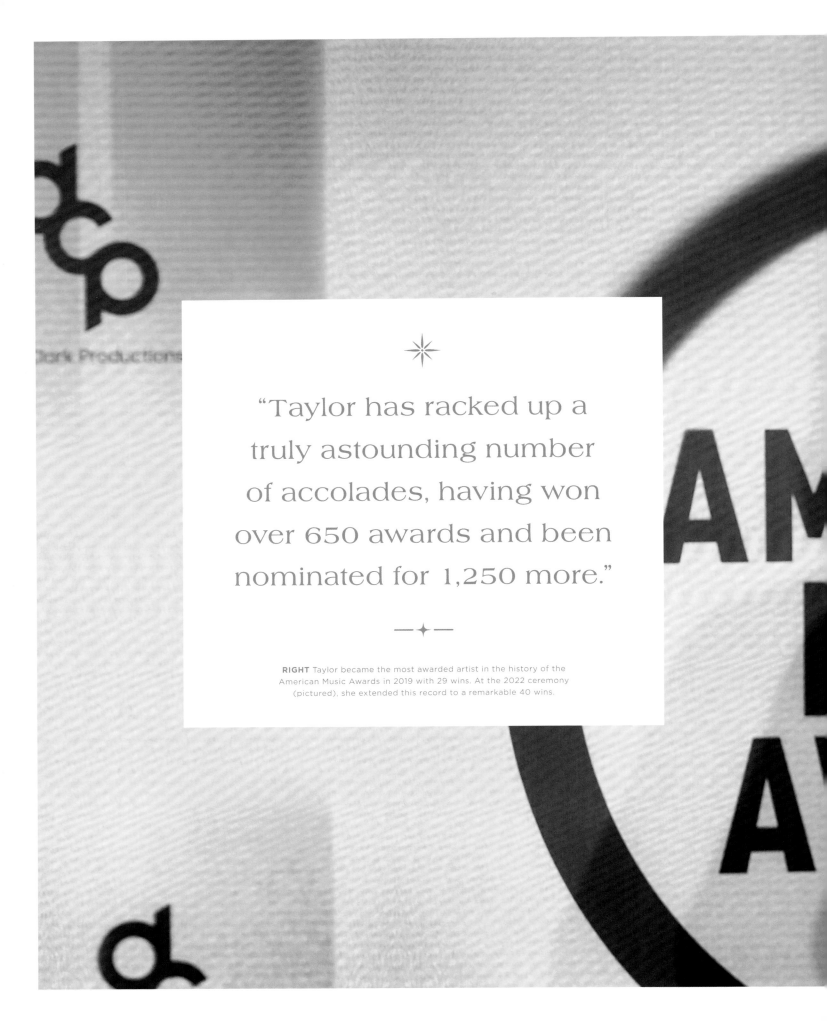

"Taylor has racked up a truly astounding number of accolades, having won over 650 awards and been nominated for 1,250 more."

RIGHT Taylor became the most awarded artist in the history of the American Music Awards in 2019 with 29 wins. At the 2022 ceremony (pictured), she extended this record to a remarkable 40 wins.

all feels to me a bit like a grand experiment. And I'm not willing to contribute my life's work to an experiment that I don't feel fairly compensates the writers, producers, artists and creators of this music. And I just don't agree with perpetuating the perception that music has no value and should be free… I thought, 'I will try this; I'll see how it feels.' It didn't feel right to me."

It's difficult to calculate exactly how much a streaming service might pay an artist per stream of a song as it's often based on a variety of factors. This can include the listener's location, whether they have a free or paid-for account, the royalty rate a specific artist may have negotiated, the relative pricing or currency conversion between different regions and so on. Streaming services have often come under fire for not paying creators a fair share for the work they produce, especially when compared to physical music sales. Spotify, in particular, is estimated to only pay around $0.004 or 0.4¢ per stream – not exactly a huge amount, when everyone including the artist, songwriter, producer and record label takes their cut! The system makes things particularly challenging for emerging artists, who may struggle to receive the many thousands of streams required to make a reasonable profit.

Taylor didn't limit her criticism to Spotify either. In June 2015, Taylor admonished Apple Music when it was discovered that they wouldn't be paying artists any royalties for streams played during users' three-month free trial period, calling it 'shocking' and 'disappointing'. Taking to Tumblr, Taylor wrote: "This is not about me. Thankfully I am on my fifth album and can support myself, my band, crew and entire management team by playing live shows. This is about the new artist or band that has just released their first single and will not be paid for its success. This is about the young songwriter who just got his or her first cut and thought that the royalties from that would get them out of debt."

Just a few days later, Apple Music backed down and announced it would pay royalties to everyone throughout its free trial period. The following week, Taylor announced that she'd be streaming her back catalogue, including new album *1989*, on the platform after all. "This is simply the first time it's felt right in my gut to stream my album," she tweeted. "Thank you, Apple, for your change of heart."

— ✦ —

David M. Benett/Getty Images.

When she then appeared in an advert for Apple in 2016 – which showed her running on (and subsequently falling off of) a treadmill while listening to an Apple Music-curated playlist called '#GYMFLOW' – it seemed their disagreement was well and truly over.

Taylor's music was put back on Spotify in June 2017. While she may not have managed to negotiate higher streaming payments for artists, she did manage to do something pretty amazing for them when signing her new record deal in 2018. After her contract with Big Machine Records ended that year, Taylor decided to leave that label and signed a new deal with Universal Music Group and Republic Records. But, unusually for a record deal, Taylor's contract proposed that the label must promise to hand over to its artists a proportion of any money it makes from any future sales of the shares it owns in Spotify – and the label agreed. Taylor said that the agreement "meant more to me than any other deal point" of her new contract, which also gave her ownership of her masters going forward. "We are headed toward positive change for creators – a goal I'm never going to stop trying to help achieve, in whatever ways I can."

As well as speaking out on the importance of artists getting fairly compensated for their work, Taylor has also spoken about how she fights to make the music industry a fairer place so that younger women are supported. When accepting *Billboard*'s Woman of the Year award in 2014, she said: "I really just feel like we need to continue to try to offer something to a younger generation of musicians, because somewhere right now your future Woman of the Year is probably sitting in a piano lesson or in a girls' choir and today – right now – we need to take care of her."

When she walked onto the *Billboard* stage once again years later to accept their Woman of the Decade award, she referred back to that 2014 speech. "I've since learned that at that exact moment, an 11-year-old girl in California really was taking piano lessons and really was in a girls' choir. And this year she has been named Woman of the Year at the age of 17. Her name is Billie [Eilish]," she reflected. "And those are the stories we need to think about every day as we do our jobs within this industry. The ones where people's dreams come true and they get to create music and play it for people. The ones where fans feel a connection to

— ✦ —

ABOVE In May 2021, Taylor became the first ever female artist (and the first non-British person) to receive the BRITs Global Icon award.

RIGHT In September 2022, Taylor was named Songwriter-Artist of the Decade at the NSAI Nashville Songwriter Awards.

"Despite Taylor's polished and confident appearance, she puts an incredible amount of pressure on herself"

music that makes their day easier, makes their night more fun, makes their love feel more sacred, or their heartache feel less isolating."

It's not just young female pop stars that Taylor has had an effect on, but young women of all levels interested in playing music. In 2018, guitar manufacturing company Fender found that 50% of new guitar sales were being driven by young women in something they called the 'Taylor Swift factor'. This suggested that, even though Taylor's music had moved away from the country-driven guitar sound which first made her famous, it's still having an effect on girls all over the world.

TAYLOR BEHIND THE SCENES

Some of the most intimate insights we've had into Taylor's life and career came from the 2020 documentary *Miss Americana*. The Lana Wilson-directed film followed Taylor over the course of several years through a range of interviews, archive footage, home videos and concert performances filmed across the making of her sixth and seventh albums, *reputation* and *Lover*.

Despite Taylor's polished and confident appearance, the film dives deep into her inner thoughts and reveals that she puts an incredible amount of pressure on herself – to make good music, to be good to her fans and, as she describes at one point, to "be thought of as good."

"My entire moral code is a need to be thought of as good," she admitted early in the film. "I was so fulfilled by approval, that that was it. I became the person who everyone wanted me to be." In one particularly revealing moment, when finding out *reputation* has not been nominated for any of the Grammys' major categories, instead of defending the album she simply stated: "This is fine. I just need to make a better record."

The documentary also saw Taylor talk candidly about the fact that, despite all her success, she isn't immune to feeling isolated or lonely. Instead, that success can sometimes create a distance between herself and those around her and leave her with difficulty finding someone to relate to. Talking about winning Album of the Year for the second

time at the Grammys, she revealed: "That was it – my life had never been better. That was all you wanted. That was all you focused on… [But] you get to the mountaintop and you look around and you're like, 'Oh God, what now?' I didn't have a partner that I'd climbed it with that I could high-five. I didn't have anyone I could talk to who could relate to… I had my mom, but I just wondered, shouldn't I have someone that I could call right now?"

She also admitted for the first time her struggle with disordered eating, something that was magnified by being in the public eye. In an honest admission in the back of a car in one scene, she explained: "I've learned over the years that it's not good for me to see pictures of myself every day… I tend to get triggered by something, whether it's a picture of me where I feel like my tummy was too big or like someone said I looked pregnant or something, and that will just trigger me to starve a little bit. Just stop eating."

Thankfully, over time, it's something she's learned to cope with. "I'm a lot happier with who I am," she added. "I don't care as much if, like, somebody points out that I have gained weight. It's just something that makes my life better, the fact that I'm a size 6 instead of a size 00."

The documentary also gives fans more insight into the dark side of fame, revealing that in one particularly grim incident a stalker broke into her apartment and slept in her bed. It was one of many incidents that led to Taylor finally be more open in her politics and speak out against Tennessee senator Marsha Blackburn, who voted against reauthorising the Violence Against Women Act, as well as voting against gay marriage.

Her decision to speak out politically was not supported by everyone on her team, who worried that it would turn the public against her and potentially threaten her safety. Taylor cited the example of The Chicks, who experienced

— ✦ —

RIGHT Taylor and Brendon Urie performing 'ME!' at the *Billboard* Music Awards in May 2019. Brendon later collaborated with Taylor once again when his band Panic! at the Disco featured on 'Electric Touch'.

BILLBOARD MUSIC AWARDS | LAS VEGAS | 01 MAY 2019

a huge backlash when they criticised President Bush over the invasion of Iraq in 2003, having their music blacklisted from country music stations and receiving death threats over their comments in America's then post-9/11 patriotic landscape. "I want to love glitter and also stand up for the double standards that exist in our society," Taylor said later in the film. "I want to wear pink and tell you how I feel about politics. I don't think those things have to cancel each other out… I need to be on the right side of history."

The film also has some heartwarming moments though, and sees Taylor discussing her relationship with former partner Joe Alwyn. Although Joe does appear briefly in the film, he's not featured too much – something Taylor admits is because of their decision to keep their relationship to themselves. "I also was falling in love with someone who had a really wonderfully normal, balanced, grounded life," she reveals. "And we decided together that we wanted our relationship to be private."

After years of sharing so much of herself with everyone and sourcing her happiness from other people's opinions of her, their relationship helped Taylor find happiness without the influence of other people. "I wasn't happy in the way I was trained to be happy," she explained. "It was happiness without anyone else's input."

During a dinner at home with her childhood friend, Abigail, they discuss friends who recently had children, and Taylor shared her thoughts on having a family of her own one day: "There's a part of me that feels like I'm 57 years old, but another part of me that's, like, definitely not ready to have kids…" she reflected. "I kind of don't really have the luxury of just figuring stuff out because my life is planned, like, two years ahead of time. In two months they'll come to me with the dates for the next tour."

Miss Americana gave audiences a chance to see the unguarded and thoughtful woman behind the cool, calm and collected celebrity that we're so used to seeing. It takes incredible resolve and serious hard work to achieve even half the things Taylor has, all while enduring the pressures of fame. But through it all, she has made it seem so easy – and that's the mark of a true superstar

— ✦ —

LEFT Taylor received an honorary doctorate from New York University in May 2022, and gave an inspiring Commencement Speech.

BELOW Pictured at the Toronto International Film Festival in September 2022. Taylor has received much critical acclaim for her skills as a director in recent years.

Valerie Macon/AFP/Getty Images.

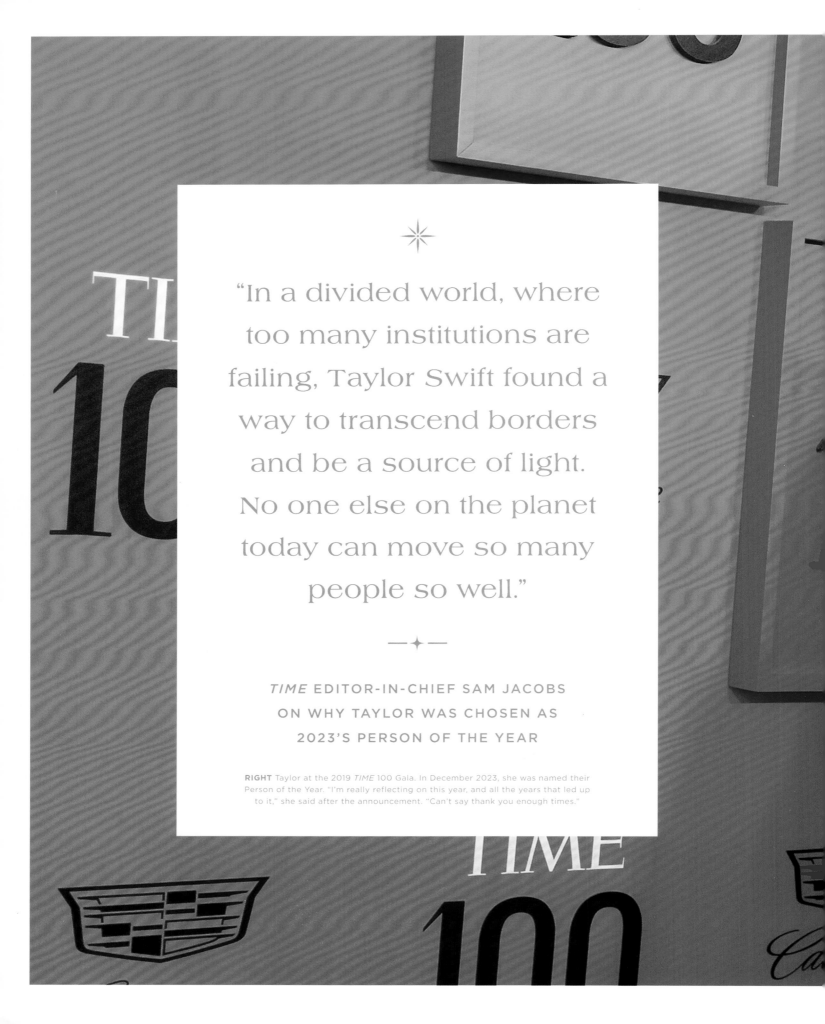

"In a divided world, where too many institutions are failing, Taylor Swift found a way to transcend borders and be a source of light. No one else on the planet today can move so many people so well."

TIME EDITOR-IN-CHIEF SAM JACOBS ON WHY TAYLOR WAS CHOSEN AS 2023'S PERSON OF THE YEAR

RIGHT Taylor at the 2019 *TIME* 100 Gala. In December 2023, she was named their Person of the Year. "I'm really reflecting on this year, and all the years that led up to it," she said after the announcement. "Can't say thank you enough times."

Quote by Sam Jacobs from Time.com. Image: Kristina Bumphrey/Starpix/Shutterstock.

CHAPTER 6

ERAS & BEYOND

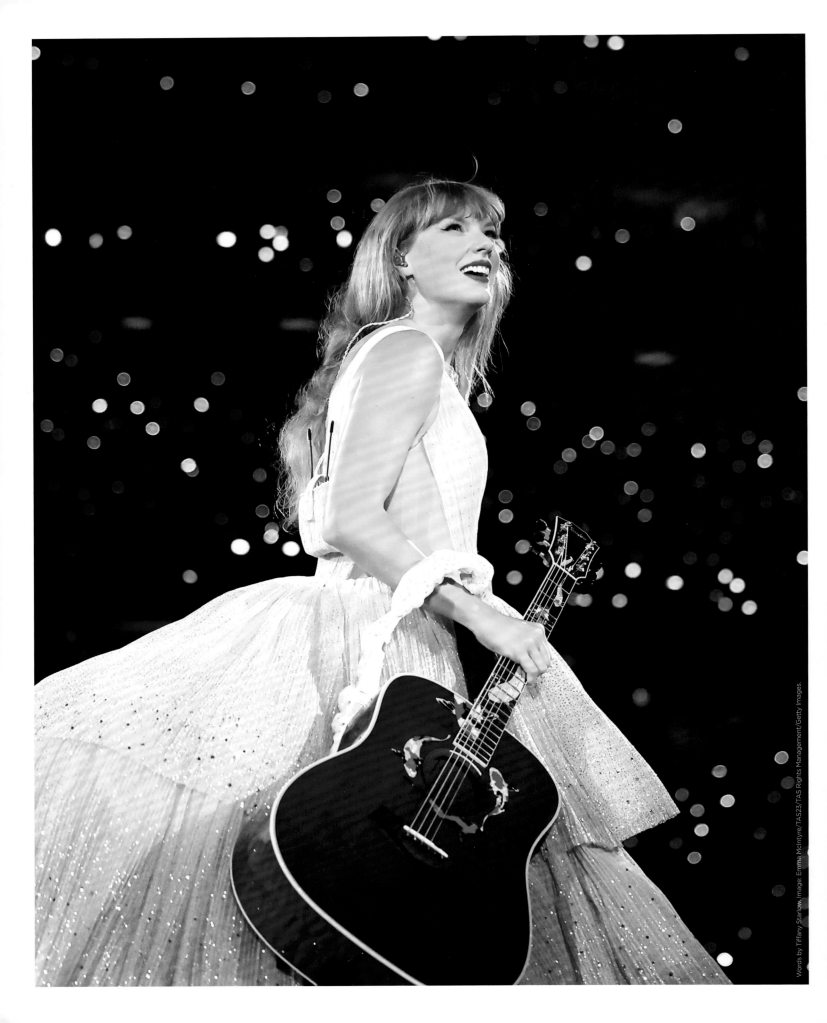

ERAS & BEYOND

With a dazzling greatest hits tour taking the world by storm, Taylor's career has reached dizzying new heights. Where will her next era take her?

The word 'icon' gets thrown around a lot these days, but when it comes to Taylor Swift it's undeniably justified. It's rare enough for a musician to maintain a successful career for nearly 20 years, but to have experienced unwavering critical and commercial acclaim – across multiple genres in a rapidly changing music industry – and *still* enjoy such unparalleled levels of global success… it's almost unheard of.

With the incredible Eras Tour taking over the world, Taylor's star power is stratospheric right now. But after a mammoth career-spanning show like that, where do you go next? Let's take a look at the Eras sensation and see what could be in store for Taylor in the years to come.

"IT'S BEEN A LONG TIME COMING…"

Cast your mind back to the summer of 2019 when *Lover* was top of the charts and hits like 'ME!', 'You Need to Calm Down' and 'The Man' filled the airwaves. Taylor was planning the Lover Fest tour in support of the new album, and was excited to get back on stage again in 2020. As part of the tour's UK dates, she was also going to be a headliner at that year's Glastonbury Festival – an unforgettable highlight in any musician's career.

Enter Covid-19. Amid the devastating global pandemic, Taylor made the sensible decision to postpone her tour dates, and later cancelled them altogether. "I'm so sad I won't be able to see you guys in concert this year, but I know this is the right decision," she announced. "Please, please stay healthy and safe. I'll see you on stage as soon as

I can but right now what's important is committing to this quarantine, for the sake of all of us."

While the world went into lockdown, Taylor kept Swifties' spirits up with the surprise releases of *folklore* and *evermore*. But as 2020 dragged into 2021, with social distancing still in place, the idea of enjoying live music as part of a crowd again seemed like a fantasy. We began to wonder if life would ever return to some kind of normal. But thanks to the tireless efforts of healthcare workers and scientists, the development and rollout of Covid vaccines meant that lockdowns could gradually start easing to allow social gatherings and events once again.

Fast forward to November 2022 and shortly after the release of *Midnights*, Taylor made an announcement on *Good Morning America*: "I wanted to tell you something that I've been so excited about for a really long time and I've been planning for ages, and I finally get to tell you I'm going back on tour. The tour is called The Eras Tour and it's a journey through all of my musical eras of my career."

Eras would be Taylor's sixth tour, and her first in five years since 2018's Reputation Stadium Tour. During that time, she had released four new albums and two re-recordings, so the usual process of theming a tour show around a single album had gone out the window, as Taylor

LEFT Taylor has said The Eras Tour "is far and away just the most electric experience of my life".

177

Natacha Pisarenko/Associated Press/Alamy.

explains during the show itself: "The way that I've always toured before […] is that I plan an album and then I do a tour," she said. "So what we found ourselves with at this point in time, there were five [sic] albums that I had not toured on, so people would come up to me and say, 'Oh, what are you gonna do now? Are you gonna do a tour that's, like, all of the albums? That's what, a three-and-a-half-hour-long show?' And I was like, 'Yes, that is exactly what we're doing. I'm going to call it The Eras Tour. See you there.'"

THE ERAS TOUR

Kicking off in Swift City (aka Glendale, Arizona, temporarily renamed in her honour) on 17 March 2023, Taylor debuted the most hotly anticipated live event of recent years. Besides the concept of a journey through her entire career, audiences didn't really know what to expect – how would Taylor incorporate so many hits and different musical styles into a single show? Spectacularly, it turns out. As if anybody had any reason to doubt her!

"I can't even go into how much I've missed you," she told her audience in what was an emotional first night of the tour. Taylor was visibly overjoyed to have that all-important live connection with her fans again. The Eras Tour also broke a long-held record that night, with 69,000 audience members making it the most attended concert by a female

artist in US history. That record was previously held by Madonna, and had stood unbeaten since 1987.

The show itself is Taylor's most ambitious concert so far. It's a near-200-minute set of more than 40 songs, with perfectly choreographed dances, moving hydraulic platforms, atmospheric set designs, dazzling lighting displays and special effects, not to mention multiple costume changes to showcase a series of stunning ensembles. All ten 'eras' of Taylor's career get a dedicated chapter, with different outfits for each one – all paying homage to her most iconic looks.

While the majority of the setlist stays the same, Taylor likes to have some surprises in store for the audience. She plays a different combination of songs during the acoustic set each night – one on guitar and one on piano – so every Eras show is unique. She has also used tour dates to make special announcements, so that fans are the first to hear about re-recordings and see music video premieres.

— ◆ —

ABOVE The Eras Tour has been a remarkable demonstration of the economic power of women.

RIGHT Taylor opens the Eras shows with the *Lover* chapter, starting with 'Miss Americana & the Heartbreak Prince'.

THE ERAS TOUR | ARIZONA | 18 MAR 2023

Image: John Shearer/TAS Rights Management/Getty Images.

> ## "To nobody's surprise, The Eras Tour has smashed records left, right and centre"

— ✦ —

Some shows have also featured surprises in the form of special guests. In addition to her stellar selection of support acts like HAIM, Phoebe Bridgers, Sabrina Carpenter and Paramore, Taylor sometimes brings other collaborators on stage to perform with her, including Jack Antonoff, Aaron Dessner and Ice Spice to name a few. At the Kansas City show in July 2023, after premiering the music video for 'I Can See You', Taylor gave the crowd another exclusive treat when the video's stars – Taylor Lautner, Joey King and Presley Cash – joined her on stage.

To nobody's surprise, The Eras Tour has smashed records left, right and centre – from ticket sales to venue milestones, and attendance figures to gross revenue. Taylor is certain to break even more as the show continues to wow crowds around the world throughout 2024. The Eras Tour has been called 'the musical event of the decade', and it is indeed hard to see how this spectacular phenomenon could be surpassed – by any other artist, that is – in terms of its sheer cultural and economic impact anytime soon.

NEW RE-RECORDINGS

As if a massive, sold-out, global stadium tour of an elaborate three-hour show wasn't enough to keep a person busy, as of February 2024 Taylor has also released two more re-recorded Taylor's Versions since Eras began.

Swifties correctly suspected *Speak Now* would be her next re-recording after 2021's *Red*, thanks to a sprinkling of hints. There are several *Speak Now* Easter eggs in the music videos for her *Midnights* singles, and the light-up wristbands that Eras audiences are given would flash purple at the end of the show. After these teases, Taylor officially announced *Speak Now (Taylor's Version)* at her first Nashville date on 5 May 2023, with the album coming out just two months later on 7 July. To celebrate the release, she extended her setlist by adding 'Long Live' to the *Speak Now* chapter of the show, which had previously just featured 'Enchanted' on its own.

There were some similar hints for *1989 (Taylor's Version)*, too. For example, when the music video for 'Bejeweled' dropped back in October 2022, eagle-eyed fans spotted

that in it, Taylor takes an elevator to the third floor, then later goes up to the fifth floor – signifying her third and fifth albums, respectively. What's more, at the end of the music video for 'I Can See You', our heroes drive away under a height restriction sign on a bridge that reads "1989 tv". Sure enough, at the final Los Angeles show of her first US leg of the tour, Taylor confirmed fans' suspicions with the announcement that *1989 (Taylor's Version)* would be released on 27 October 2023. As a final tease, throughout that show she had also been wearing new blue versions of some of her tour outfits – the colour associated with *1989*.

Both a labour of love and a matter of principle, the ambitious Taylor's Versions project is almost complete. In the meantime, we'll be keeping our eyes peeled on her new music videos and tour photos for any clues about what's next!

TAYLORMANIA

The Eras Tour generated a level of fan anticipation, excitement, hype and sheer hysteria arguably not seen since the mid-1960s when The Beatles were at the peak of their popularity. The cultural phenomenon of 'Beatlemania' saw audiences swept up into a frenzy, with the adulation and adoration from fans being unlike anything any celebrities had seen before.

It's no surprise that parallels have been drawn between the Fab Four and Taylor in this respect. From extraordinary ticket demand to record-breaking audience numbers, and a fanbase more dedicated than any other, The Eras Tour has taken Taylor's celebrity status to higher heights than ever. Fans went to extreme efforts to make sure they got their hands on Eras tickets; photos on social media showed people using a multitude of different devices all trying to get through sales queues online, while others queued around the block to try and purchase them in person. Some

— ✦ —

LEFT Eras' second act is *Fearless*, where Taylor brings back her famous 'heart hands' gesture to show her love for the fans.

"Eras generated a level of fan anticipation, excitement, hype and sheer hysteria arguably not seen since 1960s Beatlemania."

RIGHT In the *reputation* chapter, the dancers wear some of Taylor's most iconic past outfits, paying homage to the video for 'Look What You Made Me Do'.

Swifties had even camped outside venues for weeks in order to ensure they got to be in the front row.

While the impact of The Beatles was seismic in the figurative sense, with Taylor, it's literal. At the two Seattle Eras shows in July 2023, seismologists recorded activity equivalent to a magnitude 2.3 earthquake, thought to have been generated by the audience, the sound system or a combination of the two. Some truly ground-shaking stuff!

Despite the tour playing in massive stadiums, Taylor was determined to make audiences feel like they are a part of the show, too. Everyone gets given LED wristbands that twinkle, pulse and create coordinated patterns throughout the show. During 'Look What You Made Me Do' in the *reputation* chapter, for example, the wristbands generate the effect of a giant snake slithering around the stadium. The hi-tech bands aren't the only thing adorning Swifties' wrists, either. Inspired by a line from 'You're On Your Own, Kid', fans also started a tradition of making friendship bracelets to exchange with fellow audience members before the show. The trend is a fun way for strangers to connect and feel like a part of the fan community.

The intense emotions that audiences experience during an Eras performance have also had some bizarre consequences. Many fans have reported experiencing post-show amnesia – they have a fantastic time on the night,

but struggle to remember when they try to recall what actually happened. According to psychologists, this strange occurrence is likely due to fans having an overwhelming emotional and sensory experience during the show, with a lot to take in through the music, dancing, special effects, looking out for the many Easter eggs, revelling in the camaraderie of fellow audience members and so on. It's a lot for the brain to take in all at once, so not everything has a chance to get processed. Thankfully, it is thought that re-listening to the setlist could potentially make Swifties' memories come flooding back. Or perhaps seeing Eras again could help them remember…

THE ERAS CONCERT FILM

The many millions of fans who weren't able to get tickets to the live show (and, indeed, post-show amnesiacs) were delighted when Taylor announced that Eras would be coming to theatres, too. "The Eras Tour has been the most

— ✦ —

RIGHT Taylor wears a gorgeous, floaty dress in the *folklore* section. This green version was designed by Alberta Ferretti.

BELOW The stage is transformed into an ethereal woodland, complete with moss-covered piano, for the *evermore* chapter.

Matt Winkelmeyer/Getty Images.

meaningful, electric experience of my life so far and I'm overjoyed to tell you that it'll be coming to the big screen soon," she revealed on social media.

Filmed across three Los Angeles dates of the first US leg of the tour, *Taylor Swift: The Eras Tour* concert film gave cinemagoers a unique experience by combining moments from each show. Taylor took an unusual approach with the film's release by striking a deal directly with AMC Theatres in the US, rather than relying on studios to distribute it. This meant she could set the ticket prices (a symbolic $19.89, or her lucky number $13.13 for concessions) and specify the show schedules. Cutting out the 'middleman' of the studios like that was an unprecedented move, and just goes to show how Taylor's incredible star power gives her the ability to disrupt the industry, challenge the status quo and do things her own way.

On 11 October 2023, The Grove open-air mall in LA was closed off in anticipation of an influx of Swifties at the *Eras* film premiere. Thousands of fans lined the streets in the hope of seeing Taylor, who spent time walking the red carpet signing autographs and taking pictures with fans. She also visited each of the 13 cinemas at The Grove that were showing the film – to an audience of invited fans, journalists, celebrities and the Eras team – giving a speech before the screening.

"I think the fans will see – and the dancers, you'll all see – how much you are main characters in this film," she explained. "And I love you so much. I appreciate you being here because this night, it is a core memory for me and you're a part of it."

Just like the tour itself, the concert film broke records too. It became the highest-grossing concert film of all time, surpassing 2011's *Justin Bieber: Never Say Never*. Within three hours it had also broken the record for the highest number of single-day ticket pre-sales in AMC's history. In fact, *Taylor Swift: The Eras Tour* had pre-sale figures comparable to blockbuster heavyweights like *Avengers: Endgame* and *Star Wars: The Force* Awakens. As of February 2024, it has grossed a whopping $260 million worldwide, despite having a limited release of Thursday to Sunday showings.

For anyone who didn't manage to catch Eras at the cinema (and, let's face it, the millions of fans who want to

— ✦ —

ABOVE On the red carpet at the world premiere for *Taylor Swift: The Eras Tour* concert film in October 2023.

LEFT The final era of the show is *Midnights*, starting with the dreamy 'Lavender Haze'.

see it again and again), Taylor made an extended version of the film available to rent through various video on demand services. A deal was later struck with Disney+, giving the platform the exclusive rights to stream an expanded version of the show. *Taylor Swift: The Eras Tour (Taylor's Version)* includes 'cardigan' plus four extra acoustic songs that weren't featured in the other releases.

SWIFTONOMICS

In sharp contrast to her insecurities of being a monster "slowly lurching toward your favourite city", when Taylor comes to town it's a cause for celebration. And it's not just Swifties who are delighted. Big names draw in even bigger crowds, and this can provide a significant boost to the local economy.

It's not just ticket sales either. For lots of Swifties, The Eras Tour is a once-in-a-lifetime experience, treated like a vacation. The cumulative effect of fans travelling, booking accommodation, dining out, buying merchandise and so on brings a huge amount of money to the local area. According to *TIME* magazine, every $100 spent on a live performance usually leads to an average of $300 spent on these extra purchases. For The Eras Tour, however, this figure rises to an estimated $1,300-$1,500.

When Taylor played two Eras dates in Cincinnati, Ohio, the local tourist board estimated that she brought $90 million to the area thanks to the shows' 120,000 or so audience members. When she played at Glendale, Arizona, her opening night brought more revenue to local businesses than the Super Bowl held earlier that year at the same stadium.

"This isn't just about music or storytelling or brand – she is pioneering an economic model," Dan Egan from Betterment (a US-based financial advisory company) told the BBC. "Cities are constantly strapped for cash, so the impact of the Taylor Swift economy is that cities will have the revenue to invest in public infrastructure, transit, safety and planning."

In June 2023, the market research firm QuestionPro estimated that The Eras Tour had boosted the US economy to the tune of $5 billion. Bearing in mind that she was only four months into the tour by that point, it's a truly astonishing feat. Putting this into perspective, the president

— ✦ —

RIGHT Taylor with her amazing backing singers, The Starlights. From left to right: Jeslyn Gorman, Melanie Nyema, Taylor, Kamilah Marshall and Eliotte Nicole.

"Taylor revealed that her next era was right around the corner..."

of QuestionPro Research and Insights, Dan Fleetwood, explained: "If Taylor Swift were an economy, she'd be bigger than 50 countries."

The tour itself has also been a profit-making powerhouse. Before Taylor was even halfway through her 150-plus dates, the live music publication *Pollstar* reported that Eras had become the highest-grossing tour in history. It had overtaken the previous record set by Elton John's 330-show Farewell Yellow Brick Road tour, and also became the first tour ever to gross over $1 billion.

It's not just the economy that has benefitted from this mega-tour, either. In October 2023, *Forbes* reported that Taylor – at just 33 years old – had officially entered her billionaire era, with an estimated net worth of $1.1 billion. Approximately half of this comes from music royalties and touring; the first North American leg of Eras earned her nearly $200 million after taxes, and *Taylor Swift: The Eras Tour* concert film made her $35 million in the first two weeks alone. Another estimated $500 million of her earnings came from her back catalogue, the value of which has increased significantly due to her re-recording project.

What's most impressive about this feat is that, according to *Forbes*, Taylor is the first artist to reach this financial milestone solely through her music and live performances. Other musical members of the billionaire club tend to have lucrative side hustles and investments outside of the music industry – such as Rihanna's Fenty Beauty or Jay-Z's Armand de Brignac champagne brand – to boost their wealth.

In classic Taylor style, she has been finding ways to give back while on tour. In each city on the US Eras route, she made surprise donations to food banks. Not one to toot her own horn, she didn't publicise these acts of charity herself, but several of the organisations who received donations shared their stories with news outlets or on social media, thanking Taylor for her generous support.

In August 2023, it was reported by *TMZ* and *ET* that Taylor was also giving $100,000 bonuses to all of the drivers working on the first US leg of The Eras Tour, amounting to some $5 million in total. Mike Scherkenbach – whose transport company has worked with Taylor on several tours

– revealed that this bonus is around ten times the standard amount drivers would typically receive from an artist with her level of fame.

"She's giving a sum of money that is life-changing for these people," Scherkenback told *Rolling Stone*. "A lot of these drivers are not homeowners, and a lump sum like this gives you the ability to put a down payment on a home. That's what makes me really happy. That generosity is a game changer for these people."

WHAT'S NEXT?

In October 2023, Taylor released *1989 (Taylor's Version)*, leaving just two more albums to re-record: *Taylor Swift* and *reputation*. There is speculation that she has deliberately left these as the final pair – perhaps to be released simultaneously – so that she will complete the re-recording project by symbolically taking back her name and her reputation. Whether this is indeed the case, we'll have to wait and see. Either way, we can only imagine what a relief it will be for Taylor personally to be able to complete this ambitious project. She will finally own the masters to all her albums, and in doing so, will have regained control over her back catalogue.

Until at least December 2024, Taylor will be busy completing the rest of the 151-date Eras Tour. For most people, a huge world tour *and* an album re-recording project would be more than enough work to be getting on with, but Taylor Swift is not most people. At the Grammys in February 2024, she revealed that her next era was actually right around the corner. Taylor announced that her 11th studio album, called *The Tortured Poets Department*, had secretly been in the making for two years and would be coming out on 19 April 2024. She made the reveal to celebrate winning her lucky 13th Grammy trophy, and released the cover art and tracklist (including collaborations with Post Malone and Florence + the Machine) soon after.

— ✦ —

LEFT Eras' eighth set is *1989*, featuring high-energy dance routines, flame effects and pyrotechnics.

Buda Mendes/TAS23/TAS Rights Management/Getty Images.

By the time you read this, you'll be lucky enough to have heard the album, but at the time of writing we can only speculate. It's safe to say we are eagerly awaiting this next step in Taylor's musical journey.

Besides continuing her prolific music output, we also know that Taylor will be returning to the director's chair in the near future. In December 2022 it was announced that she had written an original script that will be her feature-length directorial debut, produced by Searchlight Pictures (the studio behind Oscar-winning films such as *Nomadland* and *The Shape of Water*). In a statement, Searchlight presidents David Greenbaum and Matthew Greenfield said: "Taylor is a once-in-a-generation artist and storyteller. It is a genuine joy and privilege to collaborate with her as she embarks on this exciting and new creative journey."

While details of the story and cast have been kept under wraps for now, we have already seen that Taylor is a talented director, as demonstrated by many of her music videos and *All Too Well: The Short Film*. If this new project goes well, Hollywood could provide her with another outlet for her compelling storytelling going forward.

Beyond that, who can say? There are rumours she may be appearing as the Marvel hero Dazzler in the upcoming *Deadpool 3* with her pal Ryan Reynolds, so more forays into

acting could potentially be on the horizon. But Taylor has a knack for surprising us with things even the most dedicated and eagle-eyed Swifties didn't see coming. With her love of Broadway theatricality evident in her tour shows, perhaps she will write a jukebox musical someday? We would be first in line for tickets, that's for sure!

And why should we expect her to stick solely to music and film? Taylor is one of the most influential people in the world. She's intelligent, articulate, a passionate activist with serious business savvy... could we ever see President Swift? As strange as that idea may seem, far stranger things have happened. We certainly wouldn't rule it out, and we'll be saluting our American Queen regardless!

Taylor has the extraordinary ability to defy the expectations of critics and exceed those of her fans. With her work ethic and creativity, her career truly knows no bounds. Whatever the future holds for Taylor, we'll be behind her every step of the way.

— ✦ —

ABOVE The acoustic set features surprise songs on guitar and piano.

RIGHT At the 2024 Grammys, Taylor announced that her 11th album – *The Tortured Poets Department* – would be coming soon.

"No matter what happens in life, be good to people. Being good to people is a wonderful legacy to leave behind."

LEFT Taylor performs 'Karma' for the big Eras finale, creating a party atmosphere with fireworks and confetti to bring the show to a close.